GLOBAL WARMING
ISSUES AND CHALLENGES

GLOBAL WARMING
ISSUES AND CHALLENGES

Edited by

Dr. S. Chandrasekaran

Associate Professor & Head
Post-Graduate & Research
Dept. of Economics
Government Arts College
Salem - 636 007
(INDIA)

DPH

DISCOVERY PUBLISHING HOUSE PVT. LTD.
NEW DELHI-110 002

Published by:
Namit Wasan
DISCOVERY PUBLISHING HOUSE PVT. LTD.
4383/4B, Ansari Road, Darya Ganj
New Delhi-110 002 (India)
Phone : +91-11-23279245; 23253475; 43596065
E-mail : discoverybooksindia@gmail.com
discoverypublishinghouse@gmail.com
namitwasan9@gmail.com
web : www.discoverypublishinggroup.com

Edition: **2020**

ISBN: 978-93-5056-470-7

Global Warming: ***Issues and Challenges***

Printed at:
Infinity Imaging Systems
Delhi

Foreward

Global warming is the most important challenge faced by the world of the 21st century. Its implications on food production, water supply, health and energy are the challenges that environment and social scientists are facing today. Environment degradation leads to global warming. The issue of highest importance to developing countries is reducing the vulnerability of their natural and socio-economic systems to the projected climate change. India and other developing countries will face the challenge of promoting mitigation and adaptation strategies, bearing the cost of such an effort and its implications for economic development. The most effective way to adapt to climate change is to adopt sustainable development. The research papers presented addresses these challenges.

Developing countries are faced with immediate concerns that relate to forest and land degradation, freshwater shortage, food security, air, soil and water pollution. The socio-economic and technological characteristics of different development paths will strongly affect emissions, the rate and magnitude of climate change, climate change impacts, the capability to adapt and the capacity to mitigate these changes.

India is a large developing country with nearly 700 million rural population directly depending on climate sensitive sectors and natural resources for their subsistence and livelihoods. Climate change is likely to impact all the natural eco-systems as well as socio-economic systems as indicated by UNICEF. The suggestions mentioned in the research articles when implemented can successfully prevent global warming so that the future generation can live in a perfect atmosphere. Qualitative articles published in this volume will be very useful for academicians, young and budding research scholars and policy-makers of our country.

Dr. V. S. Renukanthan

Associate Professor of Economics

Govt. Arts College

Salem -7

Preface

Good collection of select thought provoking research articles received from all over the state for the UGC sponsored State Level Seminar on 'Global Warming: *Issues and Challenges*' organized by the Post Graduate Department of Economics, Government Arts College, Salem 7 has been compiled in this book. The book has been prepared with the meticulous efforts by faculty and students of the Economics Department. In this regard, we place our sincere thanks and gratitude to the University Grants Commission for sponsoring this Seminar which has also provided a platform to bring out this book.

The theme of the seminar has been well received from subject specialists, faculty, researchers and students evident from this collection. We are grateful to the scholars for their overwhelming response. The book covers the theme of Global Warming in the backdrop of issues and challenges relating to agricultural production, inflation, human health, waste management, technological transformation and pollution. We are hopeful that this book will be helpful to economists, environmentalists, academicians, administrators and policy-makers. Our special and sincere gratitude to Discovery Publishing House Pvt. Ltd., for accepting the book for publication. Lastly, we place our sincere thanks to all those who have helped us in making this venture a success.

Dr. S. Chandrasekaran

Contents

Foreword
Preface

1. **Global Warming** **1**
Scarcity of Fresh Water
K. S. Vijayakumar

2. **Impact of Global Warming and Economic Development** **11**
Dr. A. Kubendran

3. **Impact of Climate Change on Agricultural Production at Global Level and in India** **17**
Dr. S. Gandhimathi

4. **Impacts of Global Warming** **26**
Dr. M. Manonmani

5. **A Study on Causes and Effects of Global Warming** **32**
Dr. V. Rajam, Dr. Malarvizhi.V

6. **An Empiricial Evidence of Victimising of India's Agricultural Production by Global Warming** **40**
Dr. D. Elango

7. **Environment Friendly Technologies to Save Climate** **47**
Dr. V. P. Jayalakshmi

8. **Solid Waste and Climate Change in India** **54**
N. Meera

9. **Impact of Climate Change on Paddy Production** **63**
An Emprical Evidence in Tamil Nadu
A. Palanisami

10. Domestic E-goods in Global Warming 77

DR. SRI. PA. DHEVARAJAN

11. Indian Global Warming and Climate Change in Agricultural Production 84

S. GOBI; DR. B. MUNIYANDI

12. Global Warming and Its Effects on Human Health 97

V. L. LAVANYA

13. Global Warming and the Initiatives of Environmental Awareness 104

P. MUTHUKUMAR

14. Women's Role in a Warming World 110

T.N. GEETHA

15. Impact of Global Warming in Economic Development 122

A. SENTHIL KUMAR

16. Global Warming and Agricultural Challenges 129

DR. T. SARATHY; N. SARAVANADEVI

17. Does Carbon Emission Leads to Economic Growth Rate in India 137

DR. V. S RENUKANTHAN

18. Impact of Global Warming on Agricultural Production 146

DR. S. CHANDRASEKARAN

19. Global Warming 152
Impact and Care

DR. P.AMBIGA DEVI; DR. K. SHOBHA; K. R. GOMATHI

20. Global Efforts to Control Climate Change 157

DR. C. DHANDAPANI

21. Climate Change and Food Security 168

DR. K. RAJA

22. Global Warming and Agricultural Sector 177
An Analytical Study on the Causes and Impact of Climate Change on Indian Agriculture

DR. C. RAJENDRAN

Index *185*

1

Global Warming

Scarcity of Fresh Water

K.S. Vijayakumar

Introduction

Variations in the hydrological cycle and the green house effect in the atmosphere do not predict well for the future of life on earth. The ecological effects of global warming have proved to be a great hazard and threat to our environment. If it is not controlled urgently the future generations may become victims of a disaster which could be avoided. The availability of fresh water will decrease drastically. People will be at risk of food, feed, fibre and diseases.

Global climate is warming. Climate change is real and potentially severe. Warming of the Earth's surface and lower atmosphere is caused by water vapour, carbon dioxide, and other trace gases like methane, nitrous gases etc., in the atmosphere. These naturally occurring green house gases keep ground temperatures at a global average of 15 degree Celsius. Without this natural blanket, Earth's surface would be about 30 degree Celsius colder than it is today, making the planet a freezing barren, lifeless place similar to Mars. Visible light from the Sun heats the Earth's surface. Part of this energy is

---

Associate Professor, Government Arts College (Autonomous), Salem - 7.

radiated back into the atmosphere in the form of infrared radiation, much of which is absorbed by molecules of carbon dioxide and water vapour in the atmosphere and reradiated toward the surface as more heat. Despite the name, the greenhouse effect is different from the warming in a greenhouse, where panes of glass allow the passage of visible light but hold heat inside the building by trapping warmed air. The absorption of infrared radiation causes the Earth's surface and lower atmosphere to warm more than they otherwise would, making the Earth's surface habitable.

An increase in atmospheric carbon dioxide caused by widespread combustion of fossil fuels may intensify the greenhouse effect and cause long-term climatic changes. The destruction of forests allows carbon stored in the trees to escape into the atmosphere. Likewise, an increase in atmospheric concentrations of other trace greenhouse gases such as chlorofluorocarbons, nitrous oxide, and methane resulting from human activities may also intensify the greenhouse effect. From the beginning of the Industrial Revolution through the end of the 20th century, the amount of carbon dioxide in the atmosphere increased 30 per cent and the amount of methane more than doubled.

In 1896, a Swedish chemist, Swan the Arthenius theorized that increasing amounts of carbon dioxide released into the atmosphere by coal fixed industries would cause global temperatures to rise. The first credible projections about how much green house warming might occur came in the end of mid 1960s when scientists of the Princeton University estimated that the average of global temperatures would rise by 2 degree Celsius in the 21st century.

In 1988, the UN general assembly set up the inter governmental panel on climate change (IPCC), a world wide network of 2,500 scientists to advise world leaders on global warming. The IPCC reported in June 1997, that "the balance of evidence suggests that there is a discernible human influence on global climate". Scientists are concerned that if there are increases in these gases especially carbon dioxide

Earth's atmosphere could warm up in a dangerous degree as more heat is trapped on the Earth's surface.

The 1992 Earth Summit and the 1997 Kyoto Protocol to the United Nations Framework Convention on Climate Change attempted to address the issue of global warming, but in both cases the efforts were hindered by conflicting national economic agendas and disputes between developed and developing nations over the cost and consequences of reducing emissions of greenhouse gases.

Global mean surface temperature rose a little less than 1 degree Celsius during 20th century. It does not seem all that high, but it has caused conspicuous increase in storm, cyclones, floods, droughts and raging forest fires in the last 10 years. Out of the 20 warmest years on record, 19 occurred since 1980. This is not just about how much the earth is warming, it is also about how fast it is warming. During the last 50 years the rate of global warming has nearly doubled. As per best estimates, during 21st century increase in temperature of the earth will be 3 degree to 5 degree Celsius and is expected that warming in India will be more intense.

Green House Effect

The sun is the earth's primary energy source. From this burning star we get heat which we can feel from over 152 million k.m., away. When the sunlight hits the earth surface half of it is absorbed and warms the earth and most of the rest is radiated back to the atmosphere at a longer wave length than the sunlight. Part of this longer wave lengths radiant energy is absorbed by the greenhouse gases in the atmosphere before they are lost to the space. Absorption of the radiant energy warms the atmosphere. These greenhouse gases are like a mirror and reflect black to the earth some of the heat energy which would otherwise be lost to space. This reflecting back of heat energy is green house effect. The higher the concentration of carbon dioxide in the atmosphere, the more heat energy gets reflected back to the earth. The emission of cabondioxide into the atmosphere mainly from the burning of the fossil fuels has increased over the past 50 years.

The green house effect within natural limits only, is essential for the emergence and preservation of life on this planet. Without this earth's surface would be about 30 degree Celsius colder than it is today, making the planet a freezing barren, despite the sun's constant energy supply. Hence thanks to the green house effect. Earth's atmosphere is providing us with a comfortable average temperature of 14 degree Celsius which is conductive to promotion of life on earth.

The climate change itself in many shapes and forms. Few of them are enumerated below:

- Sea level rise.
- Variability in precipitation patterns and disturbance to hydrological cycle.
- Change in frequency and of extreme events like cyclones, storms, floods and droughts.
- Change in humidity.
- Change in the growth of vegetation and forests.
- Less fresh water and less flood.
- Increase in forest fires.
- Desertification.
- Diseases.

The Hydrological Cycle

Cycle that involves the continuous circulation of water in the Earth-atmosphere system is the hydrological cycle. It is the first point in the natural phenomenon which provides fresh water to planet earth. Water is transferred from the oceans through the atmosphere to the continents and back to the oceans by means of evaporation, transpiration, precipitation, interception, infiltration, subterranean percolation, overland flow, runoff, and other complex processes. Although the total amount of water within the cycle remains essentially constant, its distribution among the various processes is continually changing. Lack or insufficiency of rain for an extended period that severely disturbs the hydrologic cycle in an area.

Earth's Water Resources

Fresh water availability is an increasing concern across the globe. Water plays a versatile role in the functioning of the biosphere. It is essential for all forms of life, plants, animals and man. Fresh water scarcity is expected to become even more a severe problem than it is today. Any of the entire range of natural waters (vapour, liquid, or solid) that occur on the Earth and that are of potential use to humans. Water scarcity is most acute in arid climates affected by droughts, the population boom, and economic development. It is estimated that by 2025, 1800 million people will be living in areas with critical water scarcity, and two-thirds of the world population might well be suffering the effects of a growing lack of clean drinking water.

Water resources include the waters of the oceans, rivers, and lakes; groundwater and deep subsurface waters and glaciers and permanent snowfields. Continuing increase in water use has led to growing concern over the availability and quality of water supplies. Although we have a plentiful supply of water in the oceans, it is not of direct use to us. We depend upon a small stock of water less than 1 per cent contained in our rivers and fresh water lakes. Even in areas where there is enough water it is often not clean enough to drink.

The vast majority of the earth's water resources are salt water with only 2.5 per cent being fresh water. Approximately 70 per cent of the fresh water available on the earth is frozen in the icecaps of Antarctica and Greenland, leaving only 0.7 per cent of total water resources world wide available for consumption. From this 0.7 per cent, roughly 67 per cent is allocated for agricultural purposes.

Even in agriculture one among the three people face water shortage and this is a major concern. Thousands of farmers commit suicide due to loss of crops and their inability to repay the agricultural loans. About 1.2 billion people or almost 1/5th of the total; population live in the areas having acute water shortage of water and another 1.6 billion and almost

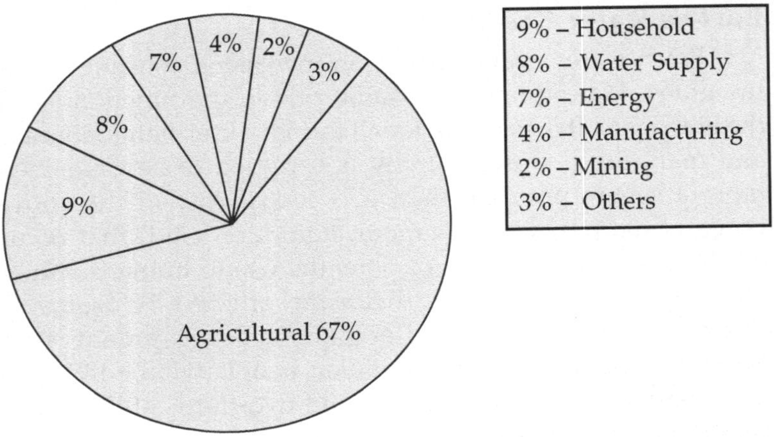

1/4th of the world population face economic water shortage where countries lack the necessary infrastructure to take water from rivers.

The reasons for the water scarcity are:

- *Over Population*: in the last century, world population has tripled. It is expected to rise to 8.9 billion by 2050. Asian cities alone are expected to grow by one billion people in the next year. Water use had been growing at more than twice the rate population increase during the last century. Increased urbanisation and concentrated population will focus on the more demand of water.
- *Climate Change:* will shrink the resources of fresh water. The more uneven distribution of precipitation in space and time due to intensification of hydrological cycle, will be leading to tremendous variability in water resources world wide. Rate of evaporation varies a great deal depending on temperature and relative humidity which impact the amount of water available to replenish ground water supplies. Evaporation, mostly from the sea and from vegetation, replenishes the humidity of the air. It is an important part of the exchange of energy in the Earth-atmosphere system that produces atmospheric motion, and therefore weather and climate. The rate of evaporation

depends on the temperature difference between the evaporating surface and the air, the relative humidity, and wind.

Water supplies are also being affected by climate change. Global warming is causing an accelerated melting of the glaciers, and there will be less glaciers in future. For example, the Himalayan glaciers feed many of the great rivers in India, China and Southeast Asia, "The full scale glacier shrinkage in the plateau regions will eventually lead to an ecological catastrophe", according to Yao Tandong of the Chinese Academy of Sciences.

More intense rainfall for small duration combined with increase evapotranspiration and increased irrigation is expected to lead the ground water depletion in a big way. Evapotranspiration is loss of water from the soil both by evaporation from the soil surface and by transpiration from the leaves of the plants growing on it. Factors that affect the rate of evapotranspiration include the amount of solar radiation, atmospheric vapour pressure, temperature, wind, and soil moisture. Evapotranspiration accounts for most of the water lost from the soil during the growth of a crop. Estimation of evapotranspiration rates is thus important in planning irrigation schemes.

Acid rain is any precipitation, including snow, that contains a heavy concentration of sulphuric and nitric acids. This form of pollution is a serious environmental problem in the large urban and industrial areas of North America, Europe, and Asia. Automobiles, certain industrial operations, and electric power plants that burn fossil fuels emit the gases sulfur dioxide and nitrogen oxide into the atmosphere, where they combine with water vapour in clouds to form sulphuric and nitric acids. The highly acidic precipitation from these clouds may contaminate lakes and streams, damaging fish and other aquatic species; damage vegetation, including agricultural crops and trees; and corrode the outsides of buildings and other structures. Though usually most severe around large urban and industrial areas, acid precipitation may also occur at great distances from the source of the pollutants.

- *Sea Level Rise:* is one of the major effects of global warming. It is happening because of the thermal expansion of the oceans, in addition to melting of the polar, Antarctica, Greenland and the land ice. As per IPCC estimates sea level may rise up to 23 m by the year 2100 in addition to inundating the vast coastal areas, it will pollute the surface and ground water and make it salty and unfit for domestic use.

Almost 40 per cent of the world population lives in coastal area less than 60 km., from the shore line. As the sea level rises, coastal communities could lose up to 50 per cent of their fresh water supplies, due to flooding of coasts world wide and a large number of coastal cities and islands will be submerged and shall vanish forever. Hydrologists have simulated how salt water will encroach into fresh water aquifers, thus converting fresh water salty and unfit for consumption. This will create scarcity and potentially reduce availability of drinking water for some of the most densely populated region of the world.

Rainfall in India and other tropical countries has gone down considerably due to global warming. Over the 20th century precipitation has mostly increased over land at high northern altitudes while decrease in other areas.

Changes in water quality and quantity due to climatic change are expected to lead to decreasing of food security and in increased vulnerability of poor rural farmers. Globally the area of land classified as very dry has more than doubled since 1970s. There has been significant decrease in water storages in mountains, glaciers and north Himalayan snow cover. It is also said that Gangotri glaciers are shrinking at the rate of 30 m per year and it is likely to vanish by year 2030. The river Ganga which draws its dry weather flow from this glacier melt, will lose its perennial nature, and will become a seasonal year beyond 2030.

The large population depends on the rivers like Brahmaputra, the Yamuna, the Indus for drinking water, cheap transportation of materials, fisheries etc. These rivers also draw their summer flow from the melt of the Himalayan glaciers. These rivers also will dry up in hot season owing to fast disappearing of glaciers. This will affect very large population of Indian subcontinent agriculturally, economically and environmentally.

Social and Economic Effect

It is now widely accepted that climate change will lead to an intensification of the global hydrological circle and will have a major impact on regional fresh water resources. In many parts of the world, variability in climatic conditions will bring about a change in precipitation and draught pattern, intensify and duration of storms, cyclones hurricanes resulting in floods, soil erosion, mass movement of land and soil moisture availability. This will affect the economic components of GDP such as agricultural productivity, Lad values and habitability of areas.

Another threat to human life resulting from climatic change is the spread of mosquito borne infectious diseases such as malaria and dengue fever as the tropical habitat of insects expands northward.

Conclusion

Water is already a major concern even without anticipated warning. Population increase and socio-economic changes, particularly in developing countries could be the major drivers of water scarcity in the next several decades. Global warming may contribute to worsening water scarcity. R.K. Pachauri, President IPCC has raised this issue in 2007 at Oslo. This is a wakeup call to the world with scientists having warned earlier that global emissions needed to be cut by 30-40 per cent from 1990 in order to stabilize the temperatures at a bearable point by 2020. However developed countries which were mandated to cut down on their emission of green house gases, 6-8 per cent by 2012, have instead increased by 9.9 per cent up to 2007. These nations are asking China, India and other developing countries to undertake reduction in their already low emission levels even as their own emission continues to rise. India's percapita emission is 1/20th of USA and 1/10th of E.U., thus the key to climate change in the hands of developed countries. They have to decide urgently to heed the advise of the international panel of scientists demanding such stronger cut over the next phase starting from 2012 for stabilize temperature.

Measures undertaken to increase water availability and to ease acute water shortages – using water more efficiently, expanding use of desalinisation, developing genetically modified crops that use less water or more saline water, and importing water – will not be sufficient to substantially change the outlook for water shortages in 2015. Many will be expensive: policies to price water more realistically are not likely to be broadly implemented within the next 15 years and subsidising water is politically sensitive for the many low-income countries short of water because their populations expect cheap water. Water has been a source of contention historically, but no water dispute has been a cause of open interstate conflict; indeed, water shortages often have stimulated cooperative arrangements for sharing the scarce resource. But as countries press against the limits of available water between now and 2015, the possibility of conflict will increase". (*Global Trends 2015,* NIC 2000-02,_National Intelligence Council, Washington, DC, December 2000, p. 27).

Our planet belongs to future generations more and as such it is a pious duty of the present generation to leave it healthy, wealthy and worthy of comfortable living.

References

1. Kanae, S (2009), Measuring and Modelling the Sustainability of Global water Resources, In Linkages of Sustainability, Strungman forum Report.
2. TERI-Adapting to Climate Change – Strategies for Water and Food Security in India.
3. ACIA 2005, Arctic Climate Impact Assessment, Scientific Report, Cambridge University Press, Cambridge.
4. Climate Change Impacts in Drought and Flood – Effected Areas: Case Studies in India – In World Bank, New Delhi, 2008.
5. Climate Change – Perspectives from India - UNDP.
6. Global Warming and the Water Crisis – Shinjiro Kanae; *Journal of Health Science.*

2 Impact of Global Warming and Economic Development

Dr. A. Kubendran

Introduction

The relations between the environment and processes of economic development have in recent years become increasingly complex. This is primarily due to the accelerated pace of economic development in many parts of the world in the last several decades, as manifested by the rapid rates at which basic statistical indicators such as gross domestic product, the volumes of industrial outputs, and the degree of urbanisation have been increasing. This phenomenon is also closely related to the institutional arrangements both in capitalist and former socialist countries, concerning the allocation of both privately owned and publicly managed resources. Since the industrial revolution, economic development has been accompanied by growth in the consumption of fossil fuels, with more and more coal, oil, and natural gas being burned by factories and electric power plants, motor vehicles, and households. The resulting carbon dioxide (CO_2) emissions have turned into the largest source

Assistant Professor, Department of Tamil, Salem Sowdeswari College, Salem - 10.

of greenhouse gases that trap the infrared radiation from the earth within its atmosphere and create the risk of global warming. Because the earth's environmental systems are so complex, the exact timing and extent to which human economic activities will change the planet's climate are still unclear.

According to the 1995 report of the Inter governmental Panel on Climate Change, by 2100 the mean global temperature could increase by 1.0–3.5 degrees Celsius and the global sea level could rise by 15–95 centimeters if current trends in greenhouse gas emissions continue. Though these may seem like minor changes, they could have multiple adverse consequences, along with some uncertain benefits. Forests and other eco-systems, unable to adapt to changing temperatures and precipitation patterns, may be damaged. People are also likely to suffer and those in poor countries may suffer the most, being less prepared to cope with the changes. Many developing countries in arid and semiarid regions may see their access to safe water worsen. Tropical diseases may spread farther to the North and flooding will likely become a bigger problem in temperate and humid regions. Food production could become easier in middle and high latitudes, in the tropics and subtropics yields will likely fall.

The amount of carbon dioxide a country emits into the atmosphere depends mainly on the size of its economy, the level of its industrialisation and the efficiency of its energy use. Even though developing countries contain most of the world's population, their industrial production and energy consumption per capita are relatively low. Until recently there has been little doubt that the primary responsibility for creating the risk of global warming lies with developed countries.

Policy Instruments for Global Warming

As argued by Bertram (1992), the institutional and policy arrangements to curtail the emission of greenhouse gases may be categorised into three types direct quantitative emission restrictions, carbon taxes and tradable emission permits. Direct quantitative emission restrictions are not only ineffective in abating the processes of global warming but also tend to obstruct the freedom of individuals only to enlarge the domain of bureaucratic control. The primary policy instruments now are environmental taxes such as carbon taxes, and markets for tradable emission permits or some other form of pricing scheme by which market institutions in a broader sense may effectively bring in to play the role of allocate mechanisms.

Global Warming

From the last 20 years, we have been warned continuously by geophysicists and meteorologists of numerous symptoms indicating that the atmospheric equilibrium is being disturbed on a global scale. The phenomenon of global warming is such a symptom apparently one of the most serious and will have enormous implications for virtually every aspect of human life on earth, affecting not only current but all future generations. The Industrial Revolution ushered in a new phase in the history of mankind. Scientific inquiries have stimulated the development of new technologies, which, in turn, have been utilised effectively by avid entrepreneurs for large-scale production of goods and services ostensibly to enrich the lives of people. In spite of many breakdowns in the process of economic development, the living standard of the average person at least one not residing in a despotic country seems now to have reached an unprecedentedly high level. However, advanced technologies and their large-scale applications, if not properly managed, tend to inflict intense and irrevocable damage to natural environments.

Forecasting Emissions Growth and Its Impact

The emissions of CO_2 end up being harmful or beneficial on balance, another substantial uncertainty is the projected size of any increase in greenhouse gas emissions over the next century. The global per capita emissions of CO_2 have been relatively stable for 20 years while the emission intensity of overall economic production has been falling. Whether the stability in per capita emissions will persist is unclear. The falling ratio of emissions to GDP reflects, in part, the increasing proportion of services, and decreasing proportion of manufacturing, in the gross national production of developed economies. This trend could be expected to accelerate in the next century as a result of continued improvements in computer and communications technology. For example, teleconferences could displace air travel for business meetings, employees may spend more time working at home and households may turn to the internet for more of their entertainment. The falling ratio of emissions to GDP may also reflect responses to higher prices for fossil fuels. Higher energy prices directly discourage energy use, for example by decreasing driving. Changes in energy prices may also temporarily reduce energy demand by disrupting the economy at the macroeconomic level. Higher energy prices also stimulate technological change aimed at improving the energy efficiency of capital equipment.

There are also extremely powerful forces tending the raise the ratio of CO_2 emissions to GDP. Developing countries, such as India and China, are turning toward low-cost manufacturing as a basis for development, attracting such industries away from the developed countries. On the one hand, since the technologies and mix of fuels currently used in the developing countries tend to produce more emissions per unit of output, a shift of manufacturing to these countries could increase world per capita emissions of CO_2. On the other hand, new manufacturing plants could incorporate advances in energy efficiency and so may contribute to the trend of declining emissions per unit of world GDP.

Improved standards of living within the developing economies China and India in particular are major potential contributors to increased CO_2 emissions per capita. Higher incomes lead to increased demand for manufactured goods. Furthermore, new transportation infrastructure, made possible by economic development, facilitates increased commercial and personal use of transportation services.

The larger emission reductions needed to stabilize the accumulation of CO_2 in the atmosphere would impose marginal and average costs far above the amounts. The differences between the marginal cost reflect the higher costs of increasing the size of emission reductions in each country. The larger reductions that for example, Canada would have to make to meet the Kyoto total without emissions trading pale into insignificance relative to the reductions that would be needed to stabilize the accumulation of CO_2 in the atmosphere. In reality, there is substantial uncertainty about the cost of achieving the level of emission reduction required to significantly retard the accumulation of CO_2 in the atmosphere. The cost would depend greatly on many factors, each of which is very difficult to forecast. These factors include: the link between emissions and CO_2 accumulation, and hence the size of the reduction.

- Future population and economic growth.
- The nature of the control regime, including the possibilities for trading quota.
- Incentives the regime generates for the development and adoption of new technologies.
- Technological developments that are independent of the control regime.
- Elasticities of substitution between energy and other inputs.

Conclusion

There are so many layers of rational skepticism about climate change policy. However, if greenhouse theory is translated into policies that succeed in stabilizing greenhouse gas concentrations in the atmosphere. Such an outcome could only be achieved through a massive and very costly reduction in current and prospective greenhouse gas emissions. An effective regime has to include developing countries. Those countries are likely to produce a rapidly growing share of world greenhouse gas emissions in coming decades. Furthermore, if developing countries are excluded from emission controls, many energy intensive industries will simply migrate from the developed to the developing world and possibly increase CO_2 emissions per unit of world GDP.

Developing countries will not agree to control greenhouse gas emissions, however, unless the costs are low enough to be acceptable given the seriousness and urgency of the other problems such countries face. The only net cost likely to be acceptable is close to zero. The inescapable conclusion is that effective controls over emissions will only be implemented at enormous cost to the taxpayers of the developed countries.

3

Impact of Climate Change on Agricultural Production at Global Level and in India

Dr. S. Gandhimathi

Climate change and agriculture are interrelated processes, both of which take place on a global scale. Global warming is projected to have significant impacts on conditions affecting agriculture, including temperature, carbon dioxide, glacial run-off, precipitation and the interaction of these elements. These conditions determine the carrying capacity of the biosphere to produce enough food for the human population and domesticated animals. The overall effect of climate change on agriculture will depend on the balance of these effects. Assessment of the effects of global climate changes on agriculture might help to properly anticipate and adapt farming to maximize agricultural production. At the same time, agriculture has been shown to produce significant effects on climate change, primarily through the production and release of greenhouse gases such as carbon dioxide, methane, and nitrous oxide, but also by altering the Earth's land cover, which can change its ability to absorb or reflect heat and light, thus contributing to radioactive forcing. Land use change such

Assistant Professor of Economics (SG/Reader), Avinashilingam Institute for Home Science and Higher Education for Women, Coimbatore - 641 043.

as deforestation and desertification, together with use of fossil fuels, are the major anthropogenic sources of carbon dioxide; agriculture itself is the major contributor to increasing methane and nitrous oxide concentrations in earth's atmosphere. In this backdrop, an attempt was made to analyse the impact of climate change on agricultural production at global level and also in India.

Due to climate change, "southern Africa could lose more than 30 per cent of its main crop, maize, by 2030. In South Asia losses of many regional staples, such as rice, millet and maize could top 10 per cent". In India, it was found that increases in temperature (by about 2°C) reduced potential grain yields in most places. Regions with higher potential productivity (such as northern India) were relatively less impacted by climate change than areas with lower potential productivity (the reduction in yields was much smaller); Overall, temperature increases are predicted to reduce rice yields. An increase of 2-4°C is predicted to result in a reduction in yields.

Climate change is a long-term change in the statistical distribution of weather patterns over periods of time that range from decades to millions of years. It may be a change in the average weather conditions or a change in the distribution of weather events with respect to an average, for example, greater or fewer extreme weather events. Climate change may be limited to a specific region, or may occur across the whole Earth. In recent usage, especially in the context of environmental policy, climate change usually refers to changes in modern climate. It may be qualified as anthropogenic climate change, more generally known as global warming or anthropogenic global warming.

Factors that can shape climate are climate forcing. These include such processes as variations in solar radiation, deviations in the Earth's orbit, mountain-building and continental drift, and changes in greenhouse gas concentrations. There are a variety of climate change feedbacks that can either amplify or diminish the initial forcing. Some parts of the climate system, such as the oceans and ice caps, respond slowly in reaction to climate forcing because of their large mass. Therefore, the climate system can take centuries or longer to fully respond to new external forcing.

Climate Change and Agricultural Production at Global Level

Despite technological advances, such as improved varieties, genetically modified organisms, and irrigation systems, weather is still a key factor in agricultural productivity, as well as soil properties and natural communities. The effect of climate on agriculture is related to variability in local climates rather than in global climate patterns. The Earth's average surface temperature has increased by 1 degree F in just over the last century. Consequently, agronomists consider any assessment has to be individually consider each local area. On the other hand, agricultural trade has grown in recent years, and now provides significant amounts of food, on a national level to major importing countries, as well as comfortable income to exporting ones. The international aspect of trade and security in terms of food implies the need to also consider the effects of climate change on a global scale.

A study published in *Science* suggests that, due to climate change, "southern Africa could lose more than 30 per cent of its main crop, maize, by 2030. In South Asia losses of many regional staples, such as rice, millet and maize could top 10 per cent". The 2001 IPCC Third Assessment Report concluded that the poorest countries would be hardest hit, with reductions in crop yields in most tropical and sub-tropical regions due to decreased water availability, and new or changed insect pest incidence. In Africa and Latin America many rain-fed crops are near their maximum temperature tolerance, so that yields are likely to fall sharply for even small climate changes; falls in agricultural productivity of up to 30 per cent over the 21st century are projected. Marine life and the fishing industry will also be severely affected in some places.

Climate change induced by increasing greenhouse gases is likely to affect crops differently from region to region. For example, average crop yield is expected to drop down to 50 per cent in Pakistan according to the UKMO scenario whereas corn production in Europe is expected to grow up to 25 per cent in optimum hydrologic conditions.

More favourable effects on yield tend to depend to a large extent on realisation of the potentially beneficial effects of carbon dioxide on crop growth and increase of efficiency in water use. Decrease in potential yields is likely to be caused by shortening of the growing period, decrease in water availability and poor verbalization.

In the long run, the climatic change could affect agriculture in several ways:

- *Productivity*, in terms of quantity and quality of crops.
- *Agricultural practices*, through changes of water use (irrigation) and agricultural inputs such as herbicides, insecticides and fertilizers.
- *Environmental effects*, in particular in relation of frequency and intensity of soil drainage (leading to nitrogen leaching), soil erosion reduction of crop diversity.
- *Rural space*, through the loss and gain of cultivated lands, land speculation, land renunciation, and hydraulic amenities.
- *Adaptation*, organisms may become more or less competitive, as well as humans may develop urgency to develop more competitive organisms, such as flood resistant or salt resistant varieties of rice.

They are large uncertainties to uncover, particularly because there is lack of information on many specific local regions, and include the uncertainties on magnitude of climate change, the effects of technological changes on productivity, global food demands, and the numerous possibilities of adaptation.

Most agronomists believe that agricultural production will be mostly affected by the severity and pace of climate change, not so much by gradual trends in climate. If change is gradual, there may be enough time for biota adjustment. Rapid climate change, however, could harm agriculture in many countries, especially those that are already suffering from rather poor soil and climate conditions, because there is less time for optimum natural selection and adaption.

Climate Change and Agricultural Production in India

In India, the agricultural sector represents 35 per cent of India's Gross National Product (GNP) and as such plays a crucial role in the country's development. Food grain production quadrupled during the post-independence era; this growth is projected to continue. The impact of climate change on agriculture could result in problems with food security and may threaten the livelihood activities upon which much of the population depends. Climate change can affect crop yields (both positively and negatively), as well as the types of crops that can be grown in certain areas, by impacting agricultural inputs such as water for irrigation, amounts of solar radiation that affect plant growth, as well as the prevalence of pests. Hence an attempt was made to analyse the vulnerability of agricultural production to climate change, with the objective of determining differences in climate change impacts on agriculture by region and by crop.

Models used to Predict Climate Change by the Indian Agricultural Research Institute (IARI)

The following models were developed by the agricultural research institute, to evaluate the impacts of changes in temperature and carbon dioxide on crops: INFOCROP, a generic growth model for various crops, was developed by IARI for optimal resource and agronomic management options. INFOCANE, a simple sugarcane growth model, was developed by IARI to measure effects on cane yield. Simple tea and coconut models were developed for tropical India and Sri Lanka. Pest damage mechanisms were coupled with INFOCROP for simulating the effect of pests. The use of this model meant that assessments could be made of the impact of climate change and its variability on incidence of pests for various crops. Interaction effects of climate changes (temperature rise, rainfall and radiation changes), with irrigation and nitrogen amounts, and agronomic management practices were established for various agro-ecologies. These were used to calculate the actual impact of climate change on agricultural production as well for suggesting agro-and resource management options for sustaining production in India.

Predicted Climate Change Effects on Agriculture

The predicted changes to agriculture vary greatly by region and crop. Findings for wheat and rice are reported here:

Wheat Production

- The study found that increases in temperature (by about 2°C) reduced potential grain yields in most places. Regions with higher potential productivity (such as northern India) were relatively less impacted by climate change than areas with lower potential productivity (the reduction in yields was much smaller).
- Climate change is also predicted to lead to boundary changes in areas suitable for growing certain crops.
- Reductions in yields as a result of climate change are predicted to be more pronounced for rain fed crops (as opposed to irrigated crops) and under limited water supply situations because there are no coping mechanisms for rainfall variability.
- The difference in yield is influenced by baseline climate. In sub tropical environments the decrease in potential wheat yields ranged from 1.5 to 5.8 per cent, while in tropical areas the decrease was relatively higher, suggesting that warmer regions can expect greater crop losses.

Rice Production

- Overall, temperature increases are predicted to reduce rice yields. An increase of 2-4°C is predicted to result in a reduction in yields.
- Eastern regions are predicted to be most impacted by increased temperatures and decreased radiation, resulting in relatively fewer grains and shorter grain filling durations.

- By contrast, potential reductions in yields due to increased temperatures in Northern India are predicted to be offset by higher radiation, lessening the impacts of climate change.
- Although additional CO_2 can benefit crops, this effect was nullified by an increase of temperature.

What are the Policy Implications of these Predictions

The policy implications for climate change impacts in agriculture are multi-disciplinary, and include possible adaptations to:

- *Food Security Policy:* To account for changing crop yields (increasing in some areas and decreasing in others) as well as shifting boundaries for crops, and the impact that this can have on food supply.
- *Trade Policy*: Changes in certain crops can affect imports/ exports, depending on the crop (this is particularly relevant for cash crops such as chilies).
- *Livelihoods*: With agriculture contributing significantly to GNP, it is critical that policy addresses issues of loss of livelihood with changes in crops, as well as the need to shift some regions to new crops, and the associated skills training required.
- *Water Policy*: Because impacts vary significantly according to whether crops are rain fed or irrigated, water policy will need to consider the implications for water demand of agricultural change due to climate change.
- *Adaptive Measures*: Policy-makers will also need to consider adaptive measures to cope with changing agricultural patterns. Measures may include the introduction of the use of alternative crops, changes to cropping patterns, and promotion of water conservation and irrigation techniques.

A Case Study on the Effect of Climate Change on Agricultural Production in India

Sushila Kau (2008), analysed the impact of climate change on agricultural production in India.

In order to study the impact of climate change on productivity, regression equations were estimated.

The results indicate that the variables of fertilizer used, human labour, actual rainfall, mean maximum temperature and mean minimum temperature, explained 73 per cent of variation in the productivity of Rice. This implies that productivity of Rice on per hectare basis is influenced by these variables. Moreover, the fertilizer use variable had a highly significant co-efficient, suggesting a significant impact of fertilizer use on productivity.

Surprisingly, the variables pertaining to actual rainfall and maximum temperature, during the growing period of the crop, had negative co-efficient, implying that these two variables had negative impact on productivity. The mean minimum temperature had a statistically significant and positive co-efficient, implying that this variable would affect the productivity of rice positively.

He also estimated regression equations for Rice crop and climate related variables, using data from various districts of Orissa state.. The results indicated that the use of fertilizer variable has a negative impact on Jowar productivity, which is not correct on theoretical grounds. However, the human labour variable has a positive and statistically significant impact on Jowar productivity. The deviation from normal rainfall had negative impact on productivity. This implies that rainfall contributes significantly in raising productivity of Jowar, which is normally a rain-fed crop. The mean maximum temperature, during the growing season of the crop had a negative implication for the crop, while the minimum temperature, during the same period, would affect the crop productivity positively. The model had better fit. In the state of Karnataka, the use of fertilizer has negative impact on the crop productivity, which is theoretically inconsistent.

The rainfall during the crop growth period has also negative co-efficient. Whereas mean maximum temperature will effect the crop positively. The results indicate that the effect of climate related variables have mixed effects on productivity of Jowar, as rainfall shows negative impact, while maximum temperature has a positive effect. However, for understanding the real effect of these variables on productivity of Jowar crop, a detailed study is required.

Need for Further Research

Due to the complex interaction of climate impacts, combined with varying irrigation techniques, regional factors, and differences in crops, the detailed impacts of these factors need to be investigated further.

Specific recommendations for further research include:

- Precision in climate change prediction with higher resolution on spatial and temporal scales.
- Linking of predictions with agricultural production systems to suggest suitable options for sustaining agricultural production.
- Preparation of a database on climate change impacts on agriculture.
- Evaluation of the impacts of climate change in selected locations.
- Development of models for pest population dynamics.

References

1. Climate Change, (2011)., http://en.wikipedia.org/wiki/Climate_change#Terminology
2. Kavi Kumar, K.S. and Jyoti Parikh (2001). "Indian Agriculture and Climate Sensitivity" Global Environmental Change, Vol. 11 (2).
3. Kaul and Sushila (2006). "Economic Analysis of Productivity of Rice Production-State-wise Analysis" presented at the 14th Annual Conference of Agricultural Economics Research Association, held during Sept. 27-28,2006 at G.B. Pant University of Agri. and Tech.., Pant Nagar, Uttaranchal.
4. Sushila Kaul (2008). Bio-economic Modelling of Climate Change on Crop Production in India, Research paper, Division of Econometrics, Indian Agricultural Statistics Research Institute, New Delhi, India.

4

Impacts of Global Warming

Dr. M. Manonmani

The phrase global warming refers to the documented historical warming of the Earth's surface based upon world wide temperature records that have been maintained by humans since the 1880s. The term global warming is often used synonymously with the term climate change, but the two terms have distinct meanings. *Global warming* is the combined result of anthropogenic (human-caused) emissions of greenhouse gases and changes in solar irradiance, while climate change refers to any change in the state of the climate that can be identified by changes in the average and/or the variability of its properties (*e.g.*, temperature, precipitation), and that persists for an extended period, typically decades or longer.

The effects could be enormous. Relative to the hectic pace of our daily life, global warming is a slow-moving problem. But that does not mean we should 'wait and see' what happens. If we wait, we may be creating an unsolvable problem,

Associate Professor in Economics, Avinashilingam Institute for Home Science and Higher Education for Women, Coimbatore - 641043, Email manomyil@yahoo.com an unstoppable climatic shift that could have devastating impacts in years to come. The majority of effects will be devastating to human and animal populations. In this paper an attempt is made to summarise the possible impacts of global warming in an economy. An insecure food supply, increased frequency and intensity of storms, rapidly rising sea levels, health hazards, environmental degradation are just a handful of the possible effects you will see in coming years.

Impact on Agriculture

Agriculture can be disrupted by wildfires and changes in seasonal periodicity, which is already taking place, and changes to grasslands and water supplies could impact grazing and welfare of domestic livestock. Increased warming may also have a greater effect on countries whose climate is already near or at a temperature limit over which yields reduce or crops fail. New crops will be able to be grown in areas that are currently too cold to support them. However, more pests and diseases may offset any benefits higher temperatures may have. Water resources will also be affected. Some reservoirs may dry up if temperature increases, especially if rainfall also decreases. Rising sea levels may pollute fresh groundwater supplies with salt water.

Impact on Health

Global warming will also affect human health. There may be more heat-related illnesses in hotter summers, and increased breathing problems as higher temperatures increase air pollution in cities, reducing air quality. The malaria mosquito may also be able to spread to other regions of the world where it is currently too cold to survive and breed.

Polar Melting

While the opening of a year-round ice free Arctic passage between the Atlantic and Pacific oceans would confer some commercial benefits, these are considerably outweighed by the negatives. Detrimental effects include loss of polar bear habitat and increased mobile ice hazards to shipping. The loss of ice albedo (the reflection of heat), causing the ocean to absorb more heat, is also a positive feedback; the warming waters increase glacier and Greenland ice cap melt, as well as raising the temperature of Arctic tundra, which then releases methane, a very potent greenhouse gas (methane is also released from the sea-bed, where it is trapped in ice-crystals called clathrates). Melting of the Antarctic ice shelves is predicted to add further to sea-level rise with no benefits accruing.

Ocean Acidification

A cause for considerable concern, there appear to be no benefits to the change in PH of the oceans. This process is caused by additional CO_2 being absorbed in the water, and may have severe destabilising effects on the entire oceanic food-chain.

Melting Glaciers

The effects of glaciers melting are largely detrimental, the principle impact being that many millions of people (one-sixth of the world's population) depend on fresh water supplied each year by natural spring melt and regrowth cycles and those water supplies – drinking water, agriculture – may fail.

Sea Level Rise

Many parts of the world are low-lying and will be severely affected by modest sea rises. Rice paddies are being inundated with salt water, which destroys the crops. Seawater is contaminating rivers as it mixes with fresh water further upstream, and aquifers are becoming polluted. Estimates of sea-level rise are feared to considerably underestimate the scale of the problem. There are no proposed benefits to sea-level rise.

Economic Concequences

Disruptions to global trade, transport, energy supplies and labour markets, banking and finance, investment and insurance, would all wreak havoc on the stability of both developed and developing nations. Markets would endure increased volatility and institutional investors such as pension funds and insurance companies would experience considerable difficulty. Developing countries, some of which are already embroiled in military conflict, may be drawn into larger and more protracted disputes over water, energy supplies or food, all of which may disrupt economic growth at a time when developing countries are beset by more egregious manifestations of climate change.

Destroying Earth

The effects could be far greater than we imagine. Global warming does not occur evenly across the world. Temperature changes have been, and will be, much more extreme in the Arctic and Antarctic. A 5 degree Fahrenheit warming for the whole world means only 1 degree at the equator, but 12 degrees at the poles. Global temperatures have already risen about .8 degrees Celsius, or 1.4 degree Fahrenheit. The arctic tundra is melting already, which may be causing an increase in methane levels in the atmosphere.

Dangerous Weather Patterns

Increased storm activity and intensity is caused by global warming. In the last several years, even insurance companies have faced regular, increasing costs from these types of storms. The ravages of global warming induced weather on the economy become yet more severe in the future. Severe drought and flooding will occur as weather pattern become more extreme. Impact on Food security.

Impact on Food Security

The price you pay for food is getting higher already as a result of global warming effects on agriculture. What's worse is that this is leaving many of the world's hungry in a desperate situation, unable to afford adequate food. In the future, it could make it so hard for humans to grow enough food that even wealthy people experience food scarcity. We depend on a predictable climate to keep our agricultural markets and our economy as a whole stable. Climate change makes our markets unstable, less efficient, and thus more expensive. Prices are increasing for a number of reasons, a few of which are not related to global warming, but global warming induced heat waves have already been shown to reduce grain harvests in India, Canada, and the U.S., significantly. Drought conditions have doubled since 1970. Many plants become less productive or will_not pollinate when it gets too hot. For all of these reasons, we should be concerned about the impacts of climate change on agriculture and food scarcity.

Effects on Animals

The danger to animals is severe as well. As sea levels rise and low land coastal areas are flooded, many animal species will be harmed. Coastal areas serve as natural hatcheries for fish and are home to a greater diversity of land and sea creatures than any other ecosystem. The flooding of coastal estuaries by rising sea levels would have dramatic effects on animals across the world.

A Hostile Planet for our Children

A relatively small rise in sea levels could have an enormous impact on people around the world.. For example, in Bangladesh, 15 million people live within 1 meter of sea level and in India, the number of people at a similar elevation is 8 million. The changes have been extreme, developing far faster than anyone foresaw, despite the fact that scientists have been predicting that significant rises in sea level could only happen decades or centuries in the future. The albedo effect of ice is believed to have had a major impact on Earth's climate over the eons and the loss of albedo could accelerate the warming of the Earth significantly. All of this means an ever more dangerous future for your kids.

The Full Effects on Humans

If the current trend continues and warming at the poles triggers a positive feedback loop whereby more carbon and methane are released into the atmosphere, then the 20-foot sea level rise could come much sooner than was previously predicted. Such a change would inundate many of the world's largest cities and much of the world's most productive farmland. The consequences could be devastating. In addition, much more dramatic sea level rises in the future are possible. If global warming catalyzes further warming and melts all of the ice in the arctic regions and at high altitudes, sea levels will rise by 230-260 feet. Earth could be drastically altered. The Earth might even come to resemble the steamy planet that was ruled by the! The harm to human populations and civilization would be incalculable.

Conclusion

Global warming affects many different facets of life on Earth. There will be winners and losers, even within a single region. But globally the losses are expected to far outweigh the benefits. Hence Global Warming is a dramatically urgent and serious problem. We don't need to wait for governments to find a solution for this problem: each individual can bring an important help adopting a more responsible lifestyle: starting from little, everyday things. It's the only reasonable way to save our planet, before it is too late. The regions that will be most severely affected are often the regions that emit the least greenhouse gases. This is one of the challenges that policy-makers face in finding fair international responses to the problem.

References

1. "Greenhouse Gases, Carbon Dioxide and Methane, Rise Sharply in 2007," Science Daily.
2. Brown, Paul, and Leipold, Gerd, Global Warning: The Last Chance for Change, Reader's Digest, Pleasantville NY, 2007, p. 131-132.
3. Sethi, Nitin (2007). "Global Warming: Mumbai to Face the Heat". Times of India.

5

A Study on Causes and Effects of Global Warming

Dr. V. Rajam*
Dr. Malarvizhi.V**

Introduction

Global warming is the observed and projected increases in the average temperature of Earth's atmosphere and oceans. The Earth's average temperature rose about 0.6° Celsius (1.1° Fahrenheit) in the 20th century. Global warming is an imminent catastrophe with irreversible consequences. The Kyoto Protocol was adopted in Kyoto, Japan on 11th December 1997 and entered into force on 16th February 2005. 180 countries have ratified the treaty to date. It aims to reduce the green house gas emissions by 5.2 per cent against the 1990 levels over the five year period 2008-12. Developed countries are categorised under Annex 1 countries and are legally bound by the protocol while the developing nations, categorised as Non Annex 1 countries, which ratify the protocol are not legally bound by it. The Kyoto Protocol has three mechanisms: *(i)* Joint Implementation (JI), *(ii)* Clean Development Mechanism (CDM) and *(iii)* International Emission Trading (IET).

* Professor, Department of Economics, Avinashilingam Deemed University for Women Coimbatore 641043.

** Assistant Professor (SS), Department of Economics, Avinashilingam Deemed University for Women Coimbatore 641043.

Rising temperatures and sea-levels in other parts of the world like United States and the U.K., but actually India is one of the most vulnerable countries when it comes to effects of global warming. India has a vast coastal line and the rising sea levels caused by global warming will cause an ecological disaster. This is according to a 1989 United Nations Environment Programme study. The uncertainties of global warming include emission rates for the various gases and their atmospheric lifetimes and concentrations; the effects of such concentrations on temperature, precipitations, and climate, especially at the regional, national and local levels; and the effects of climate change on a wide range of variables of economic significance including agriculture, sea level changes, human health, biodiversity, and basic ecological and environmental system.

Causes of Global Warming

Almost 100 per cent of the observed temperature increase over the last 50 years has been due to the increase in the atmosphere of greenhouse gas concentrations like water vapour, carbon dioxide (CO_2), methane and ozone. Greenhouse gases are those gases that contribute to the greenhouse effect. The largest contributing source of greenhouse gas is the burning of fossil fuels leading to the emission of carbon dioxide. Greenhouse gases in the atmosphere act like a mirror and reflect back to the Earth a part of the heat radiation, which would otherwise be lost to space. The higher the concentration of green house gases like carbon dioxide in the atmosphere, the more heat energy is being reflected back to the Earth. The emission of carbon dioxide into the environment mainly from burning of fossil fuels like oil, gas, petrol, kerosene, etc., has been increased dramatically over the past 50 years. Global warming causes in two ways.

Natural Causes

Natural causes are causes created by nature. One natural cause is a release of methane gas from arctic tundra and wetlands. Methane is a greenhouse gas. A greenhouse gas is a gas that traps heat in the earth's atmosphere. Another natural cause is that the earth goes through a cycle of climate change. This climate change usually lasts about 40,000 years.

Man-made Causes

Man-made causes probably do the most damage. There are many man-made causes. Pollution is one of the biggest man-made problems. Pollution comes in many shapes and sizes. Burning fossil fuels is one thing that causes pollution. Fossil fuels are fuels made of organic matter such as coal, or oil. When fossil fuels are burned they give off a green house gas called CO_2. Another major man-made cause of Global Warming is population. That means more methane because there will be more burning of fossil fuels, and more agriculture. Another source of methane is manure. Because more food is needed we have to raise food. Animals like cows are a source of food which means more manure and methane. Another problem with the increasing population is transportation. More people means more cars, and more cars means more pollution. Since CO_2 contributes to global warming, the increase in population makes the problem worse because we breathe out CO_2. Table 5.1 shows the world CO_2 emission.

Table 5.1: World CO_2, Emission By Source

Sources	World Carbon-Dioxide Emission	
	Millions Metric Tons	In percentage
Land use changes	4,000	15.5
Gas fuels	6,829	14.5
Liquid fuels	9,050	34.2
Solid fuels	5,588	32.5
Cement manufacture	-627	2.4
Gas flaring	-249	0.9
Total	**26,443**	**100**

Source: Based on World Resources Institute (1996).

Table 5.2 shows the sources of global methane emission. Agriculture and livestock together account for a little over 55 per cent.

Table 5.2: Sources of Anthropogenic Methane Emission

Sources	World Emissions (Millions Metric Tons	In percentages
Solid waste	43	16
Coal mining	36	13
Oil and Gas Production	44	16
Wet Rice Agriculture	69	26
Livestock	81	30
Total	**210**	**100**

Source: Based on World Resources Institute (1996).

Table 5.3 shows the carbon emission of various fuels per unit of energy produced. Coal is about 67 per cent more carbon-intensive per unit of energy than natural gas.

Table 5.3: Carbon Content of Fossil Fuels

Fuel	Tons Carbon Emitted Per Million BTU
Coal	25
Oil	20
Natural gas	15

BTU: British Thermal Unit

Source: Based on Watson *et al.*, (1996), Box B-2, P. 80.

The study based on world Resource Institute, showed that different regions contribute different amounts of different grew house gases. Europe and North and Central America account for 58 per cent of CO_2 from industrial sources, but only 32 per cent of methane. Asia contributes 32 per cent of industrial CO_2 and 50 per cent of methane. Other data showed that Europe plus North and Central America accounted for 5 per cent of CO_2 from deforestation, Asia 32 per cent and South America 44 per cent. The disparities are of course related to income levels and industrial/agricultural structure.

Effects of Global Warming

(i) Destruction of Eco-systems

Changing climatic conditions and dramatic increases in carbon dioxide will put our ecosystems to the test, threatening supplies of fresh water, clean air, fuel and energy resources, food, medicine and other matters we depend upon not just for our lifestyles but for our survival. Forecasts of famine, war and death paint a dire picture of climate change on our planet. Scientists are researching the causes of these changes the vulnerability of Earth not to predict the end of days but rather to help us mitigate or reduce changes that may be caused by humans. The use of more energy-efficient and sustainable resources and the adoption of other green ways of living, we may be able to make some impact on the climate change process.

(ii) Disease

Warmer temperatures along with associated floods and droughts are encouraging worldwide health threats by creating an environment where mosquitoes, ticks, mice and other disease-carrying creatures thrive. The World Health Organization (WHO) reports that outbreaks of new or resurgent diseases are on the rise and in more disparate countries than ever before, including tropical illnesses in once cold climates such as mosquitoes infecting Canadians with West Nile virus. While more than 150,000 people die from climate change-related sickness each year, everything from heat-related heart and respiratory problems to malaria are on the rise. Global warming fosters increased smog which is linked to mounting instances of asthma attacks and also advances weed growth, a bane for allergy sufferers.

(iii) Storms and Floods

During the last few years, both the United States and Britain have experienced extreme storms and flooding, costing lives and billions of dollars in damages. Between 1905 and 2005 the frequency of hurricanes has been on a steady ascent. From 1905 to 1930, there were an average of 3.5 hurricanes per year; 5.1 between 1931 and 1994; and 8.4 between 1995 and 2005. In 2005, a record number of tropical storms developed, and in 2007, the worst flooding in 60 years hit Britain.

(iv) Heat Waves

The deadly heat wave that swept across Europe in 2003, killing an estimated 35,000 people, could be the harbinger of an intense heat trend that scientists began tracking in the early 1900s. Extreme heat waves are happening two to four times more often now, steadily rising over the last 50 to 100 years, and are projected to be 100 times more likely over the next 40 years. Experts suggest continued heat waves may mean future increases in wildfires, heat-related illness and a general rise in the planet's mean temperature.

(v) Shrinking Glaciers

In the span of a century, glaciers in Montana's Glacier National Park have deteriorated from 150 to just 35. And the Himalayan glaciers that feed the Ganges River, which supplies drinking and irrigation water to 500 million people, are reportedly shrinking by 40 yards (37 meters) each year.

(vi) Rising Sea Level

Hotter temperatures mean ice glaciers, sea ice and polar ice sheets is melting, increasing the amount of water in the world's seas and oceans. Scientists are able to measure that melt water from Greenland's ice cap directly impacts people in the United States: The flow of the Colorado River has increased six fold. And scientists project that as the ice shelves on Greenland and Antarctica melt, sea levels could be more than 20 feet (6 meters) higher in 2100 than they are today. Such levels would submerge many of Indonesia's tropical islands and flood low-lying areas such as Miami, New York City's Lower Manhattan and Bangladesh.

India's Initiatives

- Signed UNFCC on 10th June 1992.
- India ratified the Kyoto protocol.
- India has a National Action Plan on Climate Change.

- National Solar Mission.
- National Mission for Enhanced Energy Efficiency.
- National Mission on Sustainable Habitat.
- National Water Mission.
- National Mission for Sustaining the Himalayan Ecosystem.
- National Mission for a 'Green India'.
- National Mission for Sustainable Agriculture.
- National Mission on Strategic Mission on Climate Change.
- India has a well developed policy, legislative regulatory and programmatic regime.
- For promotion of Energy efficiency, renewable energy, nuclear power, fuel switching, energy pricing reform addressing GHG emission.

Conclusion

The Green house gases are the main culprits of the global warming. The green house gases like carbon dioxide, methane, and nitrous oxide are playing hazards in the present times. These green house gases trap heat in earth's atmosphere and thus result in increasing the temperature of earth. The excessive emission of these gases is the major cause of global warming. India's mean surface air temperature has increased by about 0.40c during the past century. Studies based on climate model results have indicated that a 30 to 60 per cent increase in tropical cyclone activity in the north Indian Ocean may occur over the next century. This would pose and serious problems as large areas in the coastal regions have a dense population associated with fertile delta areas.

References

1. International Monetary Fund (IMF), (2008), "Climate Change and the World Economy", in World Economic Outlook April.
2. International Federation of Red Cross and Red Crescent Societies, World Disasters Report 2002, Summary of Chapter 4 on line at www.ifrc.org

3. Joshi, Vijay and Urjit Patel (2009), "India and Climate change Mitigation", in Dieter Helm and Cameron Hepburn (eds), the Economics and Politics of Climate Change Oxford University Press.
4. Lau, K.M. and Wu.H.T. (2007), "Detecting Trends in Tropical Rainfall Characteristics, 1979-2003. *International Journal of Climatology*, 27.
5. Mendelsohn, Robert, Ariel Dinar and Larry Williams (2006), "The Distributional Impact of Climate Change", *Environmental and Development Economics*, pp. 159-178.
6. Sayta Sundaram, (2010), "The Endangered Global Environment", *Southern Economist*, 49th Year of Publication, Vol. 49, No. 15.
7. Sivagaraj A and Kumar D. (2010), "Socio-Economic Damages of Climate Change in India", *Southern Economist*, 49th year of Publication, Vol. 49, No. 15, pp. 17-20.
8. Shepherd, A. and Wingham, D (2007), "Recent Sea-Level Contributions of the Antarctic and Green Land Ice Sheets, Science 315, pp. 1529-32.
9. Weir, J, (2002), "Global Warming, Earth Observatory".
10. Panagariya Arvind, (2008), "India, the Emerging Giant", New York, Oxford University Press.
11. (UNESCO 2010), "Education for All Global Monitoring Report 2010, at UN Headquarters in New York, U.S.

6

An Empiricial Evidence of Victimising of India's Agricultural Production by Global Warming

Dr. D. Elango

Introduction

Global warming is the observed and projected increases in the average temperature of Earth's atmosphere and oceans. The Earth's average temperature rose about 0.6° Celsius (1.1° Fahrenheit) in the 20th century. According to different assumption about the future behaviour of mankind, a projection of current trends as represented by a number of different scenarios gives temperature increases of about 3° to 5°C (5° to 9° Fahrenheit) by the year 2100 or soon afterwards. A 3°C or 5° Fahrenheit rise would likely raise sea levels by about 25 meters (about 82 feet). Most of the countries would be slinked in to the Ocean. Global warming is being happened by the emission of greenhouse gases. There is 72 per cent of the totally emitted greenhouse gases is carbon dioxide (CO_2), 18 per cent Methane and 9 per cent Nitrous oxide (NO_x). Carbon dioxide emissions therefore are the most important cause of global warming. CO_2 is inevitably created by burning fuels like *e.g.*, oil, natural gas, diesel, organic-diesel, petrol,

Assistant Professor, Department of Economics, Government Arts College, Coimbatore.

organic-petrol, and ethanol. The emissions of CO_2 have been dramatically increased within the last 50 years and are still increasing by almost 3 per cent each year. Climate change and agriculture are interrelated, both of which take place on a global scale. Climate will determine the Agricultural production. Global warming is projected to have significant impacts on agriculture, including temperature, precipitation and glacial run-off. These conditions determine the carrying capacity of the biosphere to produce enough food for the human population and domesticated animals.

Climate Change and Agriculture

Assessment of the effects of global climate changes on agriculture might help to properly anticipate and adapt farming to maximize agricultural production. At the same time, agriculture has been shown to produce significant effects on climate change, primarily through the production and release of greenhouse gases such as carbon dioxide, methane, and nitrous oxide, but also by altering the Earth's land cover, which can change its ability to absorb or reflect heat and light, thus contributing to radioactive forcing. Land use change such as deforestation and desertification, together with use of fossil fuels, are the major anthropogenic sources of carbon dioxide; agriculture itself is the major contributor to increasing methane and nitrous oxide concentrations in earth's atmosphere. Some of the weather projections indicated that the vulnerabilities to climate change with low to medium confidence, about a 1 to 3°C global mean temperature increase (by 2100, relative to the 1990-2000 average level) there would be productivity decreases for some cereals in low latitudes, and productivity increases in high latitudes. With medium confidence, global production potential was predicted to:

- Increase up to around 3°C.
- Very likely decrease above about 3 to 4°C.

Global Warming and India

India is a large country with all types of climates and different kinds of soil requiring different types of farming. Most of the agricultural land in India is depending on rainfall for irrigation. Some parts of the country are drought prone, the other parts are prone to flooding. For many years, parts of the country have been struggling against drought and at the same time, agricultural lands in other parts of the country are submerged due to floods. In such a country, the effects of global warming will be extreme. India has about 15 Argo-climatic zones with different types of farming methods and crops. As most of the population is dependent on agriculture and two-thirds of the country waits for the monsoon rains to aid in agriculture, any change in the frequency of the rains will affect these areas critically.

Signs of Global Warming and Climate Change

The signs of global warming are everywhere and every summer appears to be hotter than the last. Wells are running dry and the ground water has depleted. In April, all of India experienced the temperatures that are usually common in May. In Uttarakhand and Himanchal Pradesh, the states famous for their apples, the production has fallen due to temperature rise and less rain and snow. The apple belt has shifted 30 kilometers northward to higher altitudes from 9000 feet to 12,000 feet above sea level. In high altitude areas like Laddakh, with less agricultural possibilities, now it is possible to grow a larger variety of vegetables due to the increase in temperature. Houses in the foothills of the Himalayas have begun to install ceiling fans for the first time, as the average temperatures have increased. The increase in temperature has brought with them mosquitoes and house flies, which were uncommon until now. Malaria, which is found to be rare at a height of 1500 meters above sea level, is now more common in towns like Nainital, which is 2000 meters above sea level.

Farmers all over India are switching over to crops requiring less water as the rains have become irregular. As the winter rains have shifted to April in Himanchal Pradesh, they wash away the pollens of the apple flowers, thus contributing to a lower yield of the crop. Wheat production in India is decreasing every year due to the change in climate and other global warming effects. According to IARI, every

1°C increase in temperature reduces wheat production by 4-5 million tons. In high altitude areas like Leh, the tropical vegetables like bitter gourd, pumpkin, tomato, watermelon, and capsicum could not be grown locally and had to be imported from lower altitude areas in the past. It is now common to see farmers from these areas growing the same vegetables for personal as well as commercial use. In fact, the seas and the fisheries also have been affected by global warming as the Sardines are shifting from the Arabian Sea to the Bay of Bengal, traditionally not their normal habitat.

Projected Effects of Global Warming on India

The global warming effects on Indian agriculture, as projected, will be prominently on the following regions and the local population:

1. State of Rajasthan will come under drought and water scarcity will increase.
2. The Ganges will become dry as glaciers are melting and dams across the river have reduced the flow of water. It is a holy river for millions of Hindus, therefore, religious sentiments will be hurt.
3. Sea levels will increase and the Sunderbans in the Ganga valley delta will submerge.
4. Mumbai will suffer from salt water intrusion.
5. Apple crop yields will decrease further and the farmers will have to relocate to higher land resulting in further destruction of forests and higher animal encounters with humans. Already mountain leopards kill many villagers and small children along with domestic animals in the hills due to loss of forest coverage.
6. The pine forests will advance into the oak forests and destroy them. No other trees can grow underneath the pines, which would lead to a further loss of woods and fodder to the villagers.
7. Rice yields will fall in North West India.
8. Western India will suffer from a rise in sea level waters; the Runn of Kutch area will be affected.

9. In Kerala, the productivity of the forests will fall.
10. Productivity of most crops in India will fall from 10 to 40 per cent by 2100.
11. A one degree C increase in temperature will reduce the yield of soybeans, wheat, and ground nuts from 3 to 7 per cent.
12. There will be an increase in the droughts and floods in the coming future.
13. An increase in the water temperature of the sea and inland waters will affect the fish harvest, migration, and breeding as fish are not as tolerant to climate change as plants.
14. Animals will be in distress due to the heat and their reproduction will be affected.
15. Milk yields will decrease by 1.5 million tons by 2020.
16. The climate change in India is causing the glaciers in the Himalayas to melt. Therefore, a rapid release of the melted water when combined with rainfall, will lead to flash floods and landslides. It would lead to the creation of unstable lakes which can cause loss of lives and property by breaching.
17. These are the projected problems that India will suffer from in the future, and substantially, already has. In coastal Orissa, the sea has come inland 2.5 kilometers towards the Kanakpur and Satvaya region, causing about a 56 per cent loss of its mangrove vegetation.

India's Agricultural Production

There should not be any doubt that the global warming has negatively influenced much more in agricultural sector following that the economic development. The following inference indicated that the Rice, Wheat, Cereals, Pulses, Sugarcane and Oil seeds production was not significantly increased. Whereas, the crops cultivation were declined except cotton from 1964-65 to 2008-09. It is noted that the total area of crop cultivation not significantly progressive.

Table 6.1: India's Primary Agricultural Commodities Compound Growth Rates of Area, Production and Yield

(as% per annum with Base 1981 – 82 = 100)

Sl. No.	Crop	1949-50 to 1964-65			1967-68 to 2008-09		
		Area	Production	Yield	Area	Production	Yield
1.	Rice	1.21	3.50	2.25	0.50	2.46	1.99
2.	Wheat	2.69	3.98	1.27	1.20	3.69	2.46
3.	Coarse Cereals	0.90	2.25	1.23	1.41	0.67	1.99
4.	Pulses	1.72	1.41	-0.18	0.01	0.75	0.72
5.	Sugarcane	3.28	4.26	0.95	1.69	2.64	0.94
6.	Cotton	2.47	4.55	2.04	0.42	3.06	2.63
7.	Oil seeds	2.53	3.12	0.00	1.44	3.16	1.69

Source: Department of Agriculture and Co-operation.

Table 6.2: Growth Rate in Output of Various Sub-sectors of Agriculture in India

Sl. No.	Period	Cereals	Pulses and Oil Seeds	Fruits and Vegetables	Other Crops	All Crops	Live-stock	Fishery
1.	1951-52 to 1967-68	4.19	2.98	2.67	2.42	3.00	1.02	4.68
2.	1968-69 to 1980-81	3.43	0.97	4.82	2.98	3.00	3.26	3.08
3.	1981-82 to 1990-91	3.52	5.41	2.84	1.71	2.97	4.78	5.74
4.	1997-92 to 1996-97	2.36	2.92	6.07	2.18	3.09	4.00	7.05
5.	Ninth plan 1997-98 to 2001-02	1.49	-1.43	4.11	3.82	2.25	3.53	2.63
6.	Tenth plan period 2002-03 to 2006-07	1.28	4.29	2.97	3.58	2.46	3.69	3.23

Source: Eleventh five year plan document 2007-12.

The growth rate in output of sub-sectors of agriculture in India except pulses and oil seeds, the growth rate was in decline nature. It is noted that the pulses and oil seeds growth rate has declined in negative during ninth plan period. The subsequent tenth plan period has risen 4.29 per cent impressively.

Conclusion

Global warming is the observed and projected increases in the average temperature of Earth's atmosphere and oceans. If the temperature of Earth's would have increased even if 1°C, it would affect entire system of mankind and Economy. All the research study has given only their negative results on global warming. Obviously, there should not be any positive attitude especially in agricultural production might not expect high yield in coming years. The economists so far analyzing the production, irrigation, productivity and factors of production. Some time, in near future the global warming may have the factor cost and include in total cost of production.

7

Environment Friendly Technologies to Save Climate

Dr. V. P. Jayalakshmi

Industrialisation process is one of the prerequisites for accelerating the pace of economic growth and development Sustainability bridges the gulf between development and environment. Sustainable development means meeting the needs of the present without compromising the ability of future generation to fulfill their needs. Therefore environmental sustainability needs to be wrapped around the industrial development and urbanisation process with a view to attain a congenial economic growth and development.

The positive impact of Industrial Revolution is felt in terms of rising standard of living, transformation of commerce, rural to urban migration, faster growth of urbanisation, improvement in transportation and so on. Despite these positive features, the adverse impacts are in terms of unimaginable growth of urbanisation and slums, perpetuation and accentuation of urban poverty, unemployment and high incidence of environmental degradation in the form of pollution, green house effect and acid rains.

Associate Professor of Economics, Government Arts College (Autonomous), Salem - 7.

As a byproduct of industrialisation, the average temperature of Planet Earth is increasing. The chief cause of global warming is due to the burning of fossil fuels such as coal, oil and natural gas which releases carbon dioxide (CO_2) into the atmosphere. The growth of emissions of Green House Gases (GHGs) is linked to global temperature changes after some considerable time-lags.

Since green house gas emissions, especially CO_2, increased with the onset of the industrial revolution, current temperatures should have responded to these past emissions. Hence climate change is caused by concentrations, not emissions of GHGs in the atmosphere.

Emissions involve complex relationship to economic activity. The link between economic activity and emissions involves population change, rates of economic growth, the stage of development, the type of energy used to 'fuel' the economy, energy efficiency and technology.

In this context, this paper attempts:

(i) To examine the possible potentials from carbon-free sources to meet a fraction of future energy requirements.

(ii) To focus on the due share of responsibility of countries to combat the problem of global warming.

From 1965 to 2008, the use of fossil fuels has continued to grow and their share of the energy supply has increased. From 2003 to 2008 coal was the fastest growing fossil fuel.

Table 7.1: World Energy Supply, 2008

Source	**Energy (in percentages)**
Oil	33.7
Coal	26.8
Gas	20.8
Renewable sources (Hydro, Solar, wind, geo thermal power and Bio fuel)	12.9
Nuclear	5.8

Source: Climate Change Perspectives, Sunita Narain, Nov., 2009. United Nations Development Programme.

As Table 7.1 depicts that oil and coal together represented over 60 per cent of the world energy supply in the year 2008. Renewable sources able to meet only 12.9 per cent of the total energy demand.

Renewable energy is energy that comes from natural resources such as sunlight, wind, rain, tides and geo thermal heat. India has a vast supply of renewable energy sources. As of July 2009, India has 15,326 MW of installed renewable energy sources. The major sources of energy supplied in India in given in Table 7.2.

Table 7.2: Sources of Energy in India (2009)

Source	Energy Supplied (in percentages)
Coal	53
Hydro (Renewable)	25
Gas	10
Oil	1
Nuclear	3
Renewable Energy Sources	8

Source: India Energy Data, Statistics and Analysis.

Renewable power consumption grew by 15.5 per cent in 2010, the fastest rate of expansion since 1990. Global biofuel production grew 14 per cent to 59 million tonnes of oil equivalent. Geo thermal capacity increased by 1.8 per cent, solar power generating capacity increased by 73 per cent in 2010. Wind power generation went up by 24.6 per cent in the same year. The share of renewable in electricity generation is around 19 per cent with 16 per cent of global electricity coming from hydro electricity and 3 per cent from new renewables.

Apart from such renewable sources, an emerging option is to capture the CO_2 from coal power plants and bury it deep underground instead of releasing it into the atmosphere. Norway, which first began storing CO_2, has cut its emissions by almost a million tons a year. But this technology will make coal power challenging and expensive.

Many countries have started seeking energy potentials from alternative carbon free sources. Denmark and Germany had invested in solar energy despite their unfavorable geographic locations. Germany is now the largest consumer of Photovoltaic cells in the world. Brazil's attention is now on ethanol production from sugarcane, which is now a significant part of the transportation fuel in the country. France made large investments in nuclear power and to this date 75 per cent of its electricity comes from nuclear reactors. U.K., is working towards a zero energy building standard for all new housing by 2016. It is an encouraging trend that the energy use around the world has slowly shifted towards renewable energy.

At this juncture there is a wide debate going on – who should bear a greater responsibility for combating climate change? Human Development Report 2007 points out High-income OECD countries' (Organization for Economic Co-operation and Development) total emissions of CO_2 were 10,055.4 Million Metric Tonns in 1990 and 12,137.5 MMT in 2004. U.S., accounts for only 4.6 per cent of world population and is causing 22 per cent of world pollution where as India which has 17.4 per cent of world population causes only 4 per cent of CO_2 emissions. CO_2 emissions per capita from

Table 7.3: Carbon Intensity (Average Annual Growth)

Country	Average Annual Growth	Per capita Growth	Energy	Income
China	5.1	4.1	0.8	-4.3
United states	1.2	0.1	-0.1	-1.9
Russian federation	-2.4	-2.2	-0.9	-2.8
India	4.8	3.1	1.3	-1.2
Japan	0.6	0.3	-0.5	-0.5
Developing economies*	2.1	0.6	0.0	-2.0
High-income OECD	0.9	0.2	-0.4	-1.7

Source: World Development Indicators Data Files: Energy Agency: Carbon dioxide Information Analysis Centre.

*Emissions from oil Producing Economies (Excluding Russian Federation).

developing economies were less than a fourth those of developed economies in 2006 but their total emissions rate grew about twice as fast during 1990-2006.

Over the same period CO_2 emissions grew 5.1 per cent a year in china and 4.8 per cent a year in India. China became the largest emitter of CO_2 since 2006. During 1990 to 2006 developing economies' carbon energy intensity that is the ratio of CO_2 emissions per unit of energy used remain unchanged. But their carbon income intensity that is the CO_2 emitted for each unit of gross Domestic product decreased 2 per cent a year indicating greater economic productivity and energy efficiency.

The world's top five CO_2 emitters-China, the United states, Russian Federation, India, Japan all decreased their carbon income intensity in 1990-2006. Only china and India increased their carbon energy intensity because of a highest share of fossil fuel in their energy consumption.

Energy use has been increasing in china and India, both as a share of the global total and per capita.

Table 7.4: Trends in Fossil Fuel Use

Country	Energy use		Fossil Fuel	
	Share of World Energy use 2007	Average Annual Growth 1990-2007	Share of Total 2007	Average Annual Growth 1990-2007
China	16.8	4.5	86.9	0.8
United states	20.1	1.2	85.6	0.0
Russian federation	5.8	-1.3	89.3	-0.3
India	5.1	3.5	70.0	1.3
Japan	4.4	0.9	83.2	-0.1
Developing economics	52.1	2.2	79.8	0.2
High-income OECD	43.9	1.3	81.6	-0.1

Source: World Development Indicators Data Files and International Energy Agency.

Among the five economies with the highest energy consumption, India uses fossil fuels the least but its dependence on fossil fuels is growing the most, at about 1.3 per cent annually during 1990-2007.

Table 7.5: Carbon Dioxide Emissions (Million Metric Tonnes)

Country	2008	2009	2010
China	7031.9	7037.9	8240.9
U.S.	5461.0	5290.0	5492.2
India	1742.7	1629.9	2069.7
Russia	1708.6	1528.5	1688.6
Japan	1208.1	1093.8	1138.4

Source: http://en.wikipedia.org/climate change, 2010.

Owing to population growth and an urge for economic growth, energy consumption and simultaneously CO_2 emissions has been increasing at one of the fastest rates in the world. As per the above Table 7.5, China has become the first largest emitter of CO_2 followed by U.S., and India. In 2009 world energy consumption decreased for the first time as a result of financial economic crisis. But china showed no signs of slowing down during that period also. Hence even CO_2 emissions were low during 2009.

In this context the UN Framework Convention on Climate Change (UNFCC) stated that developed and developing countries have "common but differentiated responsibilities and respective capabilities". Developed countries have a higher obligation to reduce their emissions because the largest share of historical and current emissions of GHGs has originated in developed countries. Another strong point in this respect lies in the time lags that are endemic in the climate system. Present emissions of GHGs do not have immediate impacts. Warming now is caused by GHGs emitted decades ago. Each GHGs reside in the atmosphere as follows: CO_2 persists for 2 to 200 years, methane for 12 years, nitrous oxide for 114 years and perfluoromethane upwards of 50,000 years.

The per capita emissions in developing countries are still relatively low. More over developing countries want the right to expand economically like developed countries have been doing for the past 100 years. Hence their first priority is to eradicate poverty and promote socio-economic development but a low-emission development strategy is indispensable to sustainable development. With China overtaking US as a source of CO_2 emissions and with developing countries projected to be responsible for some three-quarters of primary energy demand growth by 2030, global climate change targets can only be met if developing countries start implementing strong climate policies now. If adverse impacts in 2100 are to be mitigated, action has to be taken sooner rather than later.

To conclude, global warming is a global phenomenon and therefore should be viewed globally. Externalities have been international in recent years. Hence an essential commitment of global partnership of developed and developing countries are the need of the hour to work together to save our earth. Extensive research and development programmes are needed to develop eco-friendly technologies which will enable all countries to adopt these in their effort to combat climate change.

References

1. Bharadwaj Anshu, "Carbon Counting", *Economic and Political Weekly*, Vol. XLII, No. 50, Dec. 15-21-2007.
2. Dutt Gautam, "Climate Change Negotiations at Bali", *Economic and Political Weekly*, Vol. XLIII No. 3 Jan. 19-25-2008.
3. Narain Sunita *et.al.*, "Climate Change-Perspectives from India", *United Nations Development Programme*, India, 2009.
4. Velu Suresh Kumar, "Climate Change: Its Impact on India", *Southern Economist*, Vol. 49. No. 2, May 15, 2010.
5. Economics of Climate Change, Contribution of Select Committee on Economic Affairs, Second Report of Session 2005-06 Volume I, Authority of the House of Lords, London.
6. World Development Indicators-2010. The World Bank, Report.

8

Solid Waste and Climate Change in India

N. Meera

Solid Waste Generation

Waste generation increases with population expansion and economic development. Improperly managed solid waste poses a risk to human health and the environment. Uncontrolled dumping and improper waste handling causes a variety of problems, including contaminating water, attracting insects and rodents, and increasing flooding due to blocked drainage canals or gullies. In addition, it may result in safety hazards from fires or explosions. Improper waste management also increases greenhouse gas (GHG) emissions, which contribute to climate change. This could cause serious human health and environmental consequences because a warmer climate may cause more frequent and severe heat waves, damage agriculture, and cause droughts in some places and floods in others.

There has been a considerable increase in the physical composition of municipal solid waste in India between 1996 and 2005 (Table 8.1). Considering the rapid increase in urban

MA., M.Phil., Assistant Professor, Department of Economics, Government Arts College, Salem 636 007.

Table 8.1: Physical Composition of Municipal Solid Waste in India

Composition (% to Total)

Year	Bio-degradables	Paper	Plastic/ Rubber	Metal	Glass	Rags	Others
1996	42.21	3.63	0.60	0.49	0.60	–	–
2005	47.43	8.13	9.22	0.50	1.01	4.49	4.02

Source: World Bank Institute, 2008.

population and urbanisation process, solid waste generation should also increase considerably. Taking data of metropolitan and major cities and their waste generation, the highly populated and major waste generating city is Mumbai followed by Delhi, Kolkata, Chennai and others (Table 8.2).

Table 8.2: Solid Waste Generation in Metropolitan and Major Cities in India

City	Tonnes/ Day	Estimated Population	Kg/capita
Mumbai	9786	13830884	0.71
Delhi	8203	12565901	0.65
Kolkata	7798	5138208	1.52
Chennai	4594	4616639	1.00
Bengaluru	4367	5438065	0.80
Hyderabad	3070	4068611	0.75
Ahmedabad	2287	3959432	0.58
Kanpur	2142	3221435	0.66
Surat	1629	3344135	0.49
Lucknow	1500	2750447	0.55

Source: Internal Waste Ventures, 2010.

Methods of Solid Waste Management in Some Major Cities in India

Although developed countries are striving to decouple waste generation from economic growth, overall reduction in waste generation remains a challenge, particularly in countries like India where population is increasing. Majority of the countries around the world resort any of the below mentioned methods of solid waste disposal. However, the different techniques of waste disposal in major cities of India are presented in Table 8.3. Some important methods of waste management are discussed below.

- *Recycling:* Recycling makes use of materials that otherwise would become waste by turning them into valuable resources. Recycling helps reduce greenhouse gas emissions, in part, by diverting waste from landfills. In some countries, a great deal of recycling occurs before the waste reaches the landfill. Scrap dealers buy directly from households and businesses, wastepickers or scavengers collect materials from waste bins, and waste collectors separate materials that can be sold as they load their trucks.
- *Composting:* Another form of recycling is composting – the controlled aerobic biological decomposition of organic matter, such as food scraps and plant matter, into humus, a soil-like material. Compost acts as a natural fertilizer by providing nutrients to the soil, increasing beneficial soil organisms, and suppressing certain plant diseases, thereby reducing the need for chemical fertilizers and pesticides in landscaping and agricultural activities. Organic materials often comprise a large portion of the solid waste stream, particularly in communities that rely heavily on tourism. Composting can be particularly helpful to communities managing their waste and thus reducing greenhouse gas emissions.
- *Biomethanation:* Is the formation of methane by microbes known as methanogens – Organisms capable of producing methane have been identified only from the domain Archaea, a group phylogenetically distinct from both eukaryotes and bacteria, although many live in close association with anaerobic bacteria. The production of methane is an important and widespread form of microbial metabolism. In most environments, it is the final step in the decomposition of biomass.

- *Landfill Gas (LFG):* Is the natural byproduct of the decomposition of solid waste in landfills and is composed primarily of carbon dioxide and methane. Instead of allowing LFG to escape into the air, it can be captured, converted, and used as an energy source. Using LFG helps to reduce odors and other hazards associated with LFG emissions, and it helps businesses, states, energy providers, and communities protect the environment and build a sustainable future.
- *Combustion:* Combustion is the controlled burning of waste in a designated facility to reduce its volume and, in some cases, to generate electricity. Combustion is an option for wastes that cannot be recycled or composted, and is sometimes selected by communities where landfill space is limited. While the combustion process can generate toxic air emissions, these can be controlled by installing control equipment such as acid gas scrubbers and fabric filters in combustors. Combustion of solid waste can help reduce amount of waste going to landfills. It also can reduce reliance on coal, one of the fossil fuels that produce greenhouse gases when burned.
- *Landfilling:* Uncontrolled dumping of waste can contaminate groundwater and soil, attract disease carrying rats and insects, and even cause fires. Properly designed, constructed, and managed landfills provide a safe alternative to uncontrolled dumping. For example, to protect groundwater from the liquid that collects in landfills, a properly designed landfill has an earthen or synthetic liner. As waste decomposes, it emits methane, a greenhouse gas that can also cause fires. To prevent fires, a properly designed landfill should have a way to vent, burn, or collect methane. Landfill operators can also recover this methane – thereby reducing emissions – and generate electricity from the captured gas (United States Environmental Protection Agency, 2002).
- *Leachate:* Is any liquid that, in passing through matter, extracts solutes, suspended solids or any other component

of the material through which it has passed. Leachate is a widely used term in the Environmental sciences where it has the specific meaning of a liquid that has dissolved or entrained environmentally harmful substances which may then enter the environment. It is most commonly used in the context of land-filling of industrial waste. In the narrow environmental context leachate is therefore any liquid material that drains from land or stockpiled material and contains significantly elevated concentrations of undesirable material derived from the material that it has passed through. The most common method of handling collected leachate is on-site treatment. The treated liquor is rarely of sufficient quality to be released to the environment and may be tankered or piped to a local sewage treatment facility.

- *Waste Prevention:* Waste prevention means reducing waste by not producing it. Examples of waste prevention would include purchasing durable, long-lasting goods and seeking products and packaging that are as free of toxic substances as possible. It can be as simple as switching from disposable to reusable products, or as complex as redesigning a product to use fewer raw materials or to last longer. Because waste prevention actually avoids waste generation, it is the preferred waste management activity. Overall, waste prevention conserves resources, protects the environment, and prevents the formation of greenhouse gases.

The responses to waste disposal methods adopted in various cities are not very encouraging where environment safety is concerned. The process of biomethanation, sanitary landfill, leachate treatment and LFG recovery is almost absent in all the major cities except Mumbai whereas uncontrolled dumping is the common practice. Composting, although present in all the cities, is possible only for degradable material wastes and Table 8.1 clearly shows that the composition of plastics, rubber and glass as wastes (non-degradable) are increasing over time in India and thus poses a major environment problem.

Table 8.3: Methods of Solid Waste Disposal in Metropolitan and Major Cities in India

City	Com-posting	Bio-methan-ation	Un-controlled Dumping	Sanitary Landfill	Leachate Treat-ment	LFG Recovery
Mumbai	Yes	No	Yes	Yes	Yes	Yes
Delhi	Yes	No	Yes	No	No	No
Kolkata	Yes	No	Yes	No	No	No
Chennai	Yes	No	Yes	No	No	No
Bengaluru	Yes	No	Yes	No	No	No
Hyderabad	Yes	No	Yes	No	No	No
Ahmedabad	Yes	No	Yes	No	No	No
Kanpur	Yes	No	Yes	No	No	No
Surat	Yes	No	Yes	No	No	No
Lucknow	Yes	Yes	Yes	No	No	No

Source: Internal Waste Ventures, 2010.

Typically, domestic waste from industrial countries (India also) has a high content of packaging made of paper, plastic, glass, and metal, so the waste has low density.

In many developing countries like India, domestic waste contains a large proportion of inert materials, such as sand, ash, dust, and stones, and has high moisture levels because of the high usage of fresh fruit and vegetables. These factors make the waste very dense and heavy (high weight per unit volume). So, in India, waste generation is on the increase and waste management is not very efficient. Improper waste management is not only a nuisance to people but also poses serious health and environment problems.

Climate Change and Solid Waste

Global climate change presents a significant challenge to achieving the developmental goals of countries. Extreme changes in weather such as shifts in the intensity and pattern of rainfall and variations in temperature may lower agricultural productivity, damage infrastructure, increase the incidence of vector borne diseases, cause heat related deaths, cause water scarcity, increase loss of livelihoods of people, cause displacement and migration, threaten food security, increase poverty, slow down economic growth and so on (World Bank 2010).

Even before a material or product becomes solid waste, it goes through a long cycle that involves removing and processing raw materials, manufacturing the product, transporting the materials and products to markets, and using energy to operate the product. Each of these extracting and processing activities has the potential to generate greenhouse gas emissions through energy consumption from fossil fuels. When organic waste decomposes in landfills, it generates methane, a greenhouse gas. This raises global temperatures. The Earth has already become slightly warmer in the past 100 years and will continue to become warmer. The green house gas emissions from developing countries and countries with economies-in-transition will increase in the near future due to increased urban population, increased specific (per capita) municipal solid waste generation due to improved economy and improved solid waste management practices.

There is a considerable body of literature regarding waste and climate change. The international literature on linkages between waste and climate change is largely focused on Municipal Solid Waste in developed countries, and there is limited reference or comparison to the impact of other waste streams or waste management in developing nations. The national studies rely on availability of extensive waste data sources, which is generally not the case in developing countries (UNEP, 2010). Furthermore, studies are based on domestic production, consumption, transportation, recovery and disposal processes. However, waste streams may include considerable quantities of imported products, and many countries export secondary materials to foreign recycling markets. The climate impact attributed to a domestic process may be very different to that of a foreign process.

A significant source of greenhouse emissions from India is from black carbon, methane and other air pollutants. These pollutants are emitted in large quantities in India every day from incomplete and inefficient combustion of biomass (fuel wood, crop waste and cattle dung). India's poorly managed solid wastes, inadequate sewage treatment plants; water pollution and agriculture are important sources of greenhouse gas emissions.

The waste sector is in a unique position to move from being a minor source of global emissions to becoming a major saver of emissions. Although minor levels of emissions are released through waste treatment and disposal, the prevention and recovery of wastes (*i.e.*, as secondary materials or energy) avoids emissions in all other sectors of the economy (UNEP, 2010).

Waste prevention and recycling help address global climate change by decreasing the amount of greenhouse gas emissions and saving energy (Environmental Protection Agency). Important question remains on the capacities of existing facilities for final treatment and disposal, the location and social acceptance of new facilities and as to illegal shipments of wastes. Here, the main challenge is to strengthen measures for waste minimization, especially for waste prevention and recycling, and to move further towards life cycle management of products and extended producer responsibility. This implies internalizing the costs of waste management into prices of consumer goods and of waste management services; and ensuring greater cost-effectiveness and full public involvement in designing measures (OECD Environment Directorate, 2008). Waste prevention is considered the most important action in the waste hierarchy to manage solid waste problems; however it often receives minimal priority in terms of resource allocation and effort. There is general consensus across the global waste sector that the greatest climate benefit will be achieved through improved materials management leading to waste prevention.

References

1. Da Zhu, P. U. Asnani, Chris Zurbrügg *et al.*, (2008), Improving Municipal Solid Waste Management In India: A Source Book for Policy-Makers and Practitioners, World Bank Institute, Washington.
2. Organization for Economic Cooperation and Development (OECD) (2008), Key Environmental Indicators Key Environmental Indicators Environment Directorate Paris, France.
3. United Nations Environment Programme (2010) Waste and Climate Change: Global Trends and Strategy Framework, International Environment Technology Centre, Osaka/Shiga.
4. United Nations Environment Protection Agency (2002), Solid Waste Management: A Local Challenge with Global Impacts (www.epa.gov/globalwarming/actions/waste/tools.html).

9

Impact of Climate Change on Paddy Production

An Emprical Evidence in Tamil Nadu

A. Palanisami

Introduction

Unabated global warming will reduce global agricultural capacity at least modestly by late in this century. The damages will be the most severe and begin the soonest where they can least be afforded in the developing countries like India. The losses will be much larger if carbon fertilization benefits fail to materialize, especially if water scarcity limits irrigation. Temperatures in developing countries, which are predominantly located in lower latitudes, are already closer to and beyond thresholds at which further warming will reduce rather than increase agricultural capacity. These countries tend to have less capacity to adapt the climate change. Moreover, agriculture accounts for a much larger share of GDP in developing countries than in industrial countries, so a given percentage loss in agricultural potential would impose a larger income loss in a developing country than in an industrial country.

Asst. Prof., of Economics, P.G. Department of Economics, Government Arts College, Salem - 7. Mobile: 98425 55090, Email: apalanisamia @gmail.com

Indian agriculture is facing challenges due to several factors such as increased competition for land, water and labour from non-agricultural sectors and increasing climatic variability. The latter associated with global warming will result in considerable seasonal/annual fluctuations in food production. All agricultural commodities even today are sensitive to such variability. Droughts, floods, tropical cyclones, heavy precipitation events, hot extremes and heat waves are known to negatively impact agricultural production, and farmers' livelihood. It has been projected by the recent report of the Intergovernmental Panel on climate Change (IPCC) and a few other global studies that unless we adapt, there is a probability of 10-40 per cent loss in crop production in India by 2080-2100 due to global warming. Impacts of climate change pose a serious threat to food security and need to be much better understood. In the recent past, changes in timing and amount of precipitation, extremes in temperature and widespread drought are becoming quite common in most parts of the world. The last decade, which ended with 2010, was the warmest in the past. Climate models are the main tools available for developing projections of climate change in the future. However, the presence of large uncertainties in climate models and future emission scenarios predicting long-term changes in certain climate variables, in particular in regional scales, is a challenging task that climate modelers face today. In view of the said background, the paper focuses on the Agricultural and Climatic vulnerability in Tamil Nadu by using Regression model. The paper also suggests some adaptation measures to increase resilience and agricultural productivity in India as a whole.

Review of Related Literatures

Rice is one of the most important staple food crops which is predominantly grown in the Cauvery river basin, which is also known as the rice bowl of Tamil Nadu. The research results indicate that the productivity of rice crop declines by 41 per cent for 4□C increase in temperature 8. Well calibrated and validated crop weather models could be used as an effective tool for assessing the impacts of future changes in climate. It is important to develop suitable adaptation strategies for sustaining the rice productivity to meet the demand of a growing population. In this article, two regional climate model outputs have been used to understand the climate change trends in the Cauvery river basin of Tamil Nadu for assessing the impact on rice productivity and designing suitable adaptation strategies to reduce the impacts of climate change There have been many indicators that global warming could be hurting the world food production, lowering yields and increasing prices. Turns out the warming of the planet over the past three decades has already led to a measurable reduction in crop production of wheat and maize.

Researchers from Stanford University studied global production of four major crops, maize, wheat, rice and soybean. They found the production of maize and wheat declined by 3.8 per cent and 5.5 per cent, respectively. However, the effect on rice and soybean was insignificant with gains and losses in different countries balancing each other. Understanding the impacts of past trends can help gauge the importance of near-term climate change for supply of key food commodities, says lead researcher David B Lobell, department of environmental earth system science, Stanford University in the US.

For the study the researchers analysed available data on weather patterns and crop production from 1980 to 2008. The study, published in Science Express in May 5, reported a few countryfaces-specific losses. For instance, wheat production declined in Russia by 15 per cent as well as in Turkey and Mexico. Maize production reduced in China. Such changes in production were not observed in the US. It is yet to see the warming experienced by other countries, claim the researchers.

The Intergovernmental Panel on Climate Change (IPCC) in its 2007 report had declared an increase in global average temperature by 0.18°C. The study says the warming effects on production have led to about 20 per cent increase in global market prices of the four crops. "At current market prices and global production levels, this translates to about an additional US $50 billion per year spent on food", the study states.

Indian scientists are divided on whether climate change will affect crop yield. According to Shafiq A Wani, director research of Sher-e-Kashmir University of Agricultural Sciences and Technology in Kashmir, shortage of agricultural produce directly affects markets. But R S Deshpande, director of Institute for Social and Economic Change in Bengaluru, says the decline in wheat and maize production is not big as production levels differs year to year "and should not be ascribed to one variable". However, he adds, "it does not mean we need to be complacent about climate change". The study says that rice production declined in some countries but at a global level the drop is small.

Many independent studies are being conducted in India to understand the impact of climate change on crops. One such study shows that rice production has declined in Tamil Nadu. Since 2008 the Agro Climate Research Centre of Tamil Nadu Agricultural University in Coimbatore has been assessing the impact on the state's rice production. They analysed data pertaining to temperature and rainfall on rice production in Tamil Nadu and found it is more of a climate variability than climate change.

'Rice production has been affected', says V Geethalakshmi, head of the centre. According to the study's climate projections, Tamil Nadu can experience an increase of 1.5°C towards the middle of this century. This may further increase by 2°C towards the end of the century. The rise could be mainly observed in rice-growing Cauvery delta regions. "If appropriate adaptive cultivation is not undertaken rice yield would decrease by 15 to 20 per cent by the end of the century", Geethalakshmi warns. The Global warming has resulted in 20 per cent increase in price of wheat, maize, rice and soybean, leads to food inflation.

Agriculture and allied activities, the single largest sector, acts as a growth engine by ensuring food and nutritional security to the masses besides providing raw-materials to agro-based industries and also providing employment and thereby income to the rural folk of the State and Indian Economy. Agriculture in India has undergone major structural changes in terms of the share of allied sectors in agriculture. The Share of Agriculture and allied activities in Gross Domestic Product (GDP) accounted for 17.1 per cent during 2008-09. Agriculture and logging alone had shared 16.3 per cent and the share of Forestry and Fishing accounted for 0.7 per cent and 0.8 per cent respectively. The share of agriculture sector in providing employment accounted for 52 per cent at the national level and the performance of agriculture sector is a helping hand for the growth engine of the Indian Economy.

The various studies conducted in India have shown that the surface air temperatures in India are going up at the rate of 0.4°C per hundred years, particularly during the post-monsoon and winter season. Using models, they predict that mean winter temperatures will increase by as much as 3.2°C in the 2050s and 4.5°C by 2080s, due to Greenhouse gases. Summer temperatures will increase by 2.2°C in the 2050s and 3.2°C in the 2080s. There is a noted change in the monsoons too. India is heavily dependent on the monsoon to meet its agricultural and water needs, and also for protecting and propagating its rich biodiversity. Subtle changes have already been noted in the monsoon rain patterns by scientists at IIT, Delhi. They also warn that India will experience a decline in summer rainfall by the 2050s, summer rainfall accounts for almost 70 per cent of the total annual rainfall over India and is crucial to Indian agriculture. Over 70 per cent of India's population still being agriculture dependent (either directly or indirectly), even a small impact of climate change on monsoons, erratic occurrences of floods and droughts, erratic coastal hazards such as storm surge, seawater increases etc., would enormously contribute to vulnerabilities of people. Furthermore, even relatively small climatic changes can cause large water resource problems, particularly in arid and semi-arid regions of India which will have serious implications for not only for agriculture but also for drinking water and hydro-electric power generation and overall water policy and governance. Hence, Climate change threat is no more a fiction. The earth's climate changes on global and regional scales have already affected hydrological systems and terrestrial and marine ecosystems, wetland eco-systems including mangroves and in a large measure the socio-economic life of people who depend upon these eco-systems for their livelihoods. Indeed *climate change, adaptations, vulnerability analysis and livelihood resilience* are key phrases in scientific research today. Experts across the globe are busy in assessing and understanding the damage that the man has done to Earth as we have already started harvesting the deadly repercussions climate change implications.

State of Tamil Nadu

The State of Tamil Nadu is nestled in the south eastern part of Indian peninsula between the latitudes of 8°5"N and 13°35"N and the longitudes of 76°15"E and 8 o 20". The climate in Tamil Nadu is tropical with slight variation in summer and winter temperatures. *Weather in Tamil Nadu* – Summer temperatures soars in the months between April-June and it may record up till 40° C, and the high humidity percentage in the coastal areas adds more to the discomfort Mainly tropical, the climate of Tamil Nadu is known for its warm and humid summers and moderate summers. Temperatures have known to rise almost as high as 40°C. But in the recent times the temperature increasing at all time high 40 to 44 Celsius and the rain fall is inadequate due to the climate change and further worsening situation.

Tamil Nadu shares about 4 per cent in respect of the geographical area, 7 per cent of population and 3 per cent of water resources of the country. The gross cropped area in 2008-09 accounted for about 39 per cent of the total geographical area, of which 56 per cent of the land was irrigated. The contribution of agriculture (including allied activities) of the State to the Gross State Domestic Product (GSDP) at Constant prices accounts for 9.4 per cent in 2008-

09. However, the agriculture sector ensures household food security and brings forth equity in distribution of income and wealth which would result in the reduction of poverty. For achieving the target of 4 per cent of agricultural growth as envisaged in the XI Five-year Plan Period (2007-12), agriculture is being focused in the State since 2007-08.

Land Use Pattern

Land is one of the main factors of production. The land resource constitutes the fundamental base for all human activities. The land use pattern had undergone many changes over the years. Of the total geographical area of 130.27 lakh hectares of the State, the gross cropped area was 58.24 lakh hectares during 2008-09, which worked out to 44.7 per cent. The net area sown had witnessed a gradual decline from 56.38 lakh ha. in 1950s to 56.32 lakh ha. in 1990s and further declined to 50.43 lakh ha. in 2008-09. When compared to the previous year, the net area sown had perceived a marginal decline from 50.62 lakh ha. in 2007-08 to 50.43 lakh ha. which was due to the increase in fallow lands and land put to non-agricultural uses.

Due to rise in population, urbanisation and industrialisation, the proportion of land put to non-agricultural uses was on the increase and it had marginally increased from 21.69 lakh ha. in 2007-08 to 21.73 lakh ha. in 2008-09. Of the total geographical area, forests accounts for 16.2 per cent (21.06 lakh hectares). The current fallow lands had also increased from 9.81 lakh ha. (7.5%) in 2007-08 to 10.13 lakh ha. in 2008-09 (7.8%). In the case of uncultivable land, there is no change when compared to the previous year. However, when compared to 1950s it had witnessed a decline and the reduction in the area would have gone for the promotion of forest coverage and the net area sown. The proportion of lands coming under the category of 'other fallow lands' (lands in which cultivation is not taken up for a period of 1-5 years) is on the increase from 1950s (6.6 lakh ha.) to 1990s (10.93 lakh ha.). However, it had declined marginally from 14.99 lakh ha. in 2007-08 to 14.97 lakh ha. in 2008-09 and accounts for 11.4 per cent of the State's total geographical area. The permanent pastures and other grazing lands accounts for a meager proportion of 0.8 per cent of the State's total geographical area. The area under this category in 2008-09 is more or less the same as in 2007-08. The culturable waste and miscellaneous tree crops had marginally declined from 3.47 lakh ha. and 2.61 lakh ha. in 2007-08 to 3.33 lakh ha and 2.59 lakh ha. in 2008-09 respectively.

Land Holding Size

The land holding distribution is skewed towards small and marginal farmers. Even though the small and marginal farmers occupied a major share of more than 90 per cent of the total land holdings, they were operating only about 55 per cent of the total area and the average size of holding was very meager at 0.37 hectare. The semi-medium, medium and large farmers accounting for a small proportion of 10 per cent of the holdings had operated a higher proportion of 45 per cent of the total area. The average size of holding was higher at 19.48 hectare in the case of large farmers followed by medium farmers (5.68 ha.). The overall average size of land holding had come down from 0.91 hectare in 1995-96 to 0.89 hectare in 2000-01.

The growth in the production of agricultural crops depends on many factors such as area cropped, input management and yield. The cropped area and productivity are determined by the fertility of soil, monsoon behaviour, rainfall, irrigation, availability of agricultural labourers, climatic changes, prices etc. The principal crops like paddy, coarse cereals and pulses, groundnut, cotton and sugarcane accounted for more than 60 per cent of the gross cropped area of the State.

Scenario of Paddy Production in Tamil Nadu

The State had witnessed a favourable monsoon with good precipitation during the initial months of the review year 2008-09.. The timely opening of the reservoir in the State had helped much and covered the entire area under kar, kuruvai and sornavari seasons. The samba season was kick started well in advance with favourable situation. Paddy (in terms of rice) the staple food for the State is raised more in the rice bowl districts of Thanjavur, Thiruvarur and Nagapattinam which accounted for about one fourth of the gross cropped area under paddy in the State. The area under rice cultivation almost remained stagnant in the recent years while the growth in yield rate had shown an increase in the production both at the State and at the All India level. As a result of the favorable seasonal conditions experienced in the State during the initial months of 2008-09, the State had covered more area under kar, kuruvai, sornavari, samba and thaladi seasons. However, the samba and thaladi crops were affected following heavy rains occurred during November 2008. The area under paddy rose from 17.89 lakh hectares in 2007-08 to 19.32 lakh hectares in 2008-09, the increase being 8.0 per cent. Even though, the yield rate of rice had come down from 2817 kgs./ha. in 2007-08 to 2682 kgs./ha. during 2008-09, the total production of rice had improved from 50.40 lakh tones to 51.83 lakh tones respectively.

System Rice Intensification

Rice is a staple food for more than half of the global population. The South and Southern Asian countries *viz.*, India, China, Indonesia, Bangladesh, Thailand, Vietnam, Myanmar and Philippines together account for 80 per cent of the world's rice area. At the global level, India stands first in terms of area under rice cultivation (42.4 million ha.) and occupies the second position in respect of rice production (88 million tonnes). The area under rice cultivation in India had declined from 45 million ha. in 2000-01 to 42.4 million hectares in 2008-09. The area under rice production had decreased mainly due to alarming growth of population, reduction in ground water level, aberrant weather, erratic distribution of rainfall in rice growing areas and growing interest towards the cultivation of cash crops and perennial crops. Realising the declining trend in area under rice cultivation, the State had advocated the System Rice Intensification (SRI). Under SRI, the high yielding ADT varieties like 35, 36, 42, 43, 45 and 48, white ponni, CR 1009, ASD 18, ASD 19 and CO 43 and the low tillering varieties

ADT 37, TKM 9 and ASD 16 are cultivated during the kuruvai, early samba and navarai season except samba and thaladi season. Under SRI cultivation, the States were given a subsidy of Rs. 5000/- per hectare was given to the farmers as a motivation to switch over from the conventional method of cultivation to this new technique. The area under SRI demonstration had increased from 4.21 lakh ha. in 2007-08 to 5.38 lakh ha. in 2008-09 in the State. The average yield per hectare had also gone up to 7634 kgs. Thus, it is a welcome feature that the SRI method of cultivation being adopted in the State is cost effective and saves water from 30 to 40 per cent and increases production, boost up with high yield rate which could bring food security in the near future.

Application of Inputs in Paddy Cultivation

The agricultural production and productivity depend on the input supply like quality seeds, fertilizer, plant protection chemicals, adoption of pest management techniques, credit management along with adequate rainfall and assured irrigation facilities.

Rainfall

The overall area coverage, production and productivity depend on the timely onset of the monsoon and good precipitation in the State. The State had experienced favourable seasonal conditions during the initial period of 2008-09. The opening of the Mettur dam for irrigation on the scheduled date of 12th June of there view year (2008) had helped to cover more area under kar, kuruvai, and sornavari seasons. Even though the samba season started with favourable condition, it was affected by heavy rain during November 2008. The temporal and spatial spread of rainfall during South West Monsoon had augmented much to store water in the reservoirs in the State. During 2008-09, the rainfall received in the South West monsoon and North East monsoon was encouraging and more than the normal level. However, it had witnessed a dip by 2.6 per cent as compared to the previous year actual (341.6 mm). The precipitation during north east monsoon was satisfactory in 2008-09 and registered an increase of 7.2 per cent over the previous year 2007-08. Total rainfall (1023.1mm) during 2008-09 was found to be higher than the normal level.

Chemical Fertilizer

The application of chemical fertilizer is advocated in the State based on soil test. The balanced use of chemical fertilizers would help in improving the productivity of crops. The consumption of chemical fertilizer was comparatively more than biofertilizers. The green revolution technologies and development of various irrigation sources had resulted in increasing the level of fertilizer consumption. Likewise, the production and the use of bio-fertilizer in the State is gaining momentum. However, the application of fertilizer is imperative for stepping up the yield rate in Agriculture Sector The actual consumption of chemical fertilizers *viz.* Nitrogen, Prosperous and Potash in the State was found to be in the ratio of 2:1:1 as against the conventionally accepted ratio of 4:2:1 which indicates that there was an imbalance in the use of chemical fertilizers. The total consumption of chemical fertilizer had increased from 10.76 laky tones in 2007-08 to 12.65 lakhs tones, registering an increase of 17.6 per cent, of which the consumption of Nitrogen and Potash accounted for an increase of 19 per cent each and phosphorous by 11.8 per cent during 2008-09.

Table 9.1: Trends in Paddy Production, Rainfall and Chemical Fertilizer use in Tamil Nadu

Details	2006-07	2007-08	2008-09
Paddy (Production in lakh tones);	66.11	**50.40**	**51.83**
Rainfall (in mm)	859.7	**1164.4**	**1023.1**
Chemical fertilizer Per hectare (kgs.)	187	**166**	**166**

Source: 1. Season and Crop Reports, Department of Economics and Statistics, Chennai - 6.

Source: 2. Policy Note on Agriculture 2009-10, Department of Agriculture, Chennai - 5.

To find the impact of climate change on paddy production the following regression model is used. In this Model the relationship between production of paddy and rainfall, use of chemical fertiliser specified by a regression equation. The specifications used for model are as follows:

$$Y= a+b_1X_1+b_2X_2+U$$

Where,

Y = Paddy production

a = constant

X_1 = Rainfall (in mm)

X_2 = Chemical Fertiliser

U = error term

Discussion and Interpretation of Regression Results

Running a regression of paddy production (Y) on Rainfalls (X_1) and application of chemical fertilizer (X_2) and using the information found in the Table 9.2, the fitted regression equation is as follows:

Table 9.2: Estimated Regression Results for Paddy Production, Ranifall and Chemical Fertiliser

Sl. No.	Variables	Co-efficient	'T' Value
1.	Constant	441.878	0.1717
2.	Rainfall	-36.89	-0.0059*
3.	Chemical Fertiliser	-57.20	-0.4672
4.	R^2	0.579	
5.	Adjust R^2	0.561	
6.	F-Value	4.50	

Source: Calculated By Using Spss.

$$\hat{Y} = 441.87-36.89(X_1)- 57.20(X_2)$$

Considering the Fitted equation coefficient (-37 lakhs tons of paddy) for the rainfall (X_1) as a explanatory variable, which indicates that If an extra one millimeter rainfall declines 37 lakhs tons of paddy production will decrease, and vice versa. It shows that the amount of rainfall decreases the precipitation due to global warming which causes the climate change and in turn reduces the paddy yield. Further considering the co-efficient of chemical fertilizer (-57.20) as a explanatory variable, which shows the expected sign but is not significant. It is indicating that the prolonged usage of chemical fertilizers would result in deterioration of soil health and directly affect the food production.

Policy Implications for Decision-Makers

The following policy implications are recommended for the decision-makers in tamil nadu as whole State. They are as follows:

1. In case of paddy the climate variables (rainfall and temperature) are influencing the productivity of paddy. From the adaptation point of view, area and yield responses in paddy are more indicative of behaviour of the decision makers. Adaptation practices due to climate changes are higher in paddy as the major food grain.
2. The traditional cropping systems suitable for the areas should be re-introduced at least as a crop rotation measure.. Also, interventions should be grouped under the short-term and long-term categories. The short-term interventions normally range from the adoption of crop varieties to water management practices to suit the climate changes, suitable irrigation methods and soil moisture conservation measures etc.
3. The National Rural Employment Guarantee Scheme (NREGS) can be integrated with tank rehabilitation programmes.. Given the priority for investment, the policy makers can start from the highly vulnerable areas and then move to less vulnerable areas for minimizing the impact of climate change.
4. The State should implement Agricultural Technology Management system vigorously to Support the State extension programme.
5. State should advocate the usage of bio-fertilizer for ecologically protected farming. With the application of bio-fertilizers, the fertility and health of the soil could be sustained and plant growth could be promoted.

6. National Agricultural Insurance Scheme (NAIS) and plant protection measures should be implemented and create awareness among the farmers in the State on war fed basis.
7. The organic manure would improve the water holding capacity of the soil and Enhance microbial activity and also help in augmenting the nutrient absorption capacity of the crop. The application of organic manure is promoted through cultivation of green manure crops, application of vermi composting blue green algae, azolla and biofertilizers. Further, the micro nutrients help in sustaining the fertility and health of the soil.

References

1. Geethalakshmi, V. A. Lakshmanan, D. Rajalakshmi, R. Jagannathan, Gummidi Sridhar, A. P. Ramaraj, K. Bhuvaneswari, L. Gurusamy and R. Anbhazhagan, "Climate Change Impact Assessment and Adaptation Strategies to Sustain Rice Production in Cauvery Basin of Tamil Nadu," Current Science, Vol. 101, No. 3, 10 August 2011, pp. 342-347.
2. Indu Mathi. S., Climate Change Hits Food Production, Issue: June 30, 2011.
3. Jayaseelan. I, "Climate Change Impacts in Tamil Nadu", Submitted to on the Frontlines of Climate Change 26/08/09.
4. Naresh Kumar, S. P. K. Aggarwal, Swaroopa Rani, Surabhi Jain, Rani Saxena and Nitin Chauhan, "Impact of Climate Change on Crop Productivity in Western Ghats, Coastal and Northeastern Regions of India," Current Science, Vol. 101, No. 3, 10 August 2011, pp. 332-342.
5. Palanisami. K., Kakumanu. K.R., *et al.*, "Impacts of Climate Change on Agricultural Production: Vulnerability and Adaptation in the Godavari River Basin, India", Clima Water Report, No. 4, December 2010.
6. William R. Cline, "Global Warming and Agriculture Impact Estimates by Country", July 2007, 250 pp, ttp://www.peterson institute.org/publications/author_bio.cfm?author_id=44.
7. Data Sources: I. Department of Economics and Statistics, Chennai - 6 II. Policy Note on Agriculture 2009-10, Department of Agriculture, Chennai - 5.

10

Domestic E-Goods in Global Warming

Dr. Sri. PA. Dhevarajan

Introduction

Global Warming is not an issue of an individual house but an alarm to every human being in the Universe. No one could blame any other living being or Nature for this burning issue because human mind is the only cause and reason for this entire atmosphere pollution. Global warming is not a minor issue than can be ignored but a deadly threat to everyone under the Sun. Global warming means the increase of Earth's average surface temperature due to the effect of greenhouse gases such as carbon dioxide, water vapor, nitrous oxide, methane and emissions from burning fossil fuels or from deforestation which trap heat that would otherwise escape from earth. The heat and light from the sun is produced in the centre of the sun. This layer is called core. Here the temperature of the sun is about 27,000,000F. When the temperature reaches the surface of the earth's atmosphere, it

M.A., M.A., M.Phil., TCY, Ph.D., Asst. Prof. of English, PG and Research Department of English, Government Arts College (Autonomous), Salem - 636 007. Mobile: 09361551808. E-mil: spdevan@gmail.com is about 10,000F after the transmission of many layers. This is called radiant energy from which we get light and heat.

Greenhouse gasses that prevail on the earth's atmosphere collect too much heat and light from the sun and pass enormous heat and light to the earth where no atmosphere is available to filter it. As a result people, animals, and plants would die because the heat is too strong. This is like when heat is trapped inside a car. The car gets hotter when it is out in the parking lot. The heat and light from the sun gets into the car through windows but cannot get back out. This is what the greenhouse effect does to the earth. The heat and light reaches the atmosphere but it cannot get out. As a result, the temperature rises and people, plants and animals have to undergo excess light and heat. This would cause a break in the chain of food and cause even death.

Marine Degradation

The oceans are affected by global warming in other ways. Many things related to the ocean are linked to global warming. One thing that causes global warming is harming and killing algae in the ocean. Algae is a producer which makes food for other animals through photosynthesis, like grass. This floating green algae is food to many consumers in the ocean like small fish, crabs, some whales and many other animals. Fewer algae is a problem which causes less food for many creatures in the sea and simultaneously deficiency of sea food for human being. This killing of plant and trees would cause global warming which is linked to acid rain. Acid rain kills everything it touches. Plants collect carbon dioxide that living being breathes out and they give back oxygen that to breathe in. With fewer trees and other plants such as algae, there is less air for us and more green house gas is sent into the air. It is very important to protect the trees to stop the greenhouse effect and to inhale air to be alive.

Environment degradation may boost the occurrence and concentration of severe climate events, such as floods, famines, heat waves, tornados, and twisters. Other consequences may comprise of higher or lower agricultural outputs, glacier melting, lesser summer stream flows, genus extinctions and rise in the ranges of disease vectors. As an effect of global warming species like golden toad, harlequin frog of Costa Rica has already become extinct. There are number of species that have a threat of disappearing soon as an effect of global warming. As an effect of global warming various new diseases have emerged lately. These diseases are occurring frequently due to the increase in earth's average temperature since the bacteria can survive better in elevated temperatures and even grow faster when the conditions are favorable. The global warming is extending the distribution of mosquitoes due to the increase in humidity levels and their frequent growth in warmer atmosphere. Various diseases due to ebola, hanta and machupo virus are expected due to warmer climates.. Likewise, earlier one more team of scientists reported that the in a single year Greenland witnessed 32 glacial earthquakes between 4.6 and 5.1 on the Richter scale. This is a disturbing sign and points that a huge destabilisation that may now be in progress deep within the second biggest accretion of ice on the planet. This ice would be enough to raise sea level 20 feet worldwide if it broke up and slipped into the sea.

The garbage also pollutes the environment. When it is thrown away, it goes to the landfills. When it is burnt, it produces enormous amount of green gases in the air that causes global warming worse. This particular gas carbon dioxide, CO_2, collects light and heat (radiant energy) produced by the sun and this makes the earth warmer. Human beings have increased the CO_2 concentration in the atmosphere by about thirty per cent, which is an extremely significant increase, even on inter-glacial timescales. It is believed that human beings are responsible for this because the increase is almost perfectly correlated with increases in fossil fuel combustion, and also due other evidence, such as changes in the ratios of different carbon isotopes in atmospheric CO_2 that are consistent with 'anthropogenic' (human caused) emissions. Some other factors that cause air pollution are:

- *Ozone:* This is the basic element for smog. It is produced when many polluted chemicals combined together. It causes many health issues related to lungs. It can affect plants and causes eye-problems.
- *Volatile Organic Compounds (VOC):* VOCs are smog formers, formatted when fuel is burnt. It can cause cancer and affects plants.
- *Nitrogen Dioxide:* It is formed by burning sources of energy like gas, oil, coal and fossil fuels. It can cause respiratory problems, acid rain and affects trees. It can eat away the buildings and idols.
- *Carbon Monoxide:* This is formatted from burning sources of energy and causes blood vessel problems and affects respiratory failures.
- *Particulate Matter:* This source can plow and burn down the fields. It causes breathing trouble, damages the lungs and causes death.
- *Sulfur Dioxide:* This chemical is produced in the process of making paper and metal. It can cause damage to lungs buildings ans statues and causes acid rain.
- *Lead:* This substance is available in paint, lead storage batteries, leaded gasoline, and smelters and in few metals. It causes nerve problems, digestive problems and affects the brain.

Methane is more than 20 times as effectual as CO_2 at entrapping heat in the atmosphere. Methane is obtained from resources such as rice paddies, bovine flatulence, bacteria in bogs and fossil fuel manufacture. When fields are flooded, anaerobic situation build up and the organic matter in the soil decays, releasing methane to the atmosphere. The main sources of nitrous oxide include nylon and nitric acid production, cars with catalytic converters, the use of fertilizers in agriculture and the burning of organic matter. Another cause of global warming is deforestation that is caused by cutting and burning of forests for the purpose of residence and industrialisation.

Domestic E-Goods

One more thing that causes global warming is electrical pollution. Electricity causes pollution in many ways, some worse than others. In most cases, fossil fuels are burnt to create electricity. Fossil fuels are made up of dead plants and animals. Some examples of fossil fuels are oil and petroleum. Many pollutants (chemicals that pollute the air, water and land) are sent into the air when fossil fuels are burnt. Some of these chemicals are called greenhouse gasses. Petroleum is used for transportation, making electricity and it causes a lot of pollution.

Very important electrical pollution that every house does is using domestic electrical and electronic goods which cause severe damage to the environment unknowingly. No house is left out without Television, washing machine, refrigerator, air conditioner, computer, electrical and electronics play goods etc. These domestic E-goods produce a lot of heat and affect the environment. The continuous use of these E-goods produce large amount of heat and pollution to the entire atmosphere. The average temperature of a city is heavier than a village because no tree or water resource is there to minimize the effect. Carpooling is yet another reason for this environmental degradation because the mode of transportation has become a symbol of status. Fuel emission is the deadly threat now a day. Usage of non-eco friendly things and goods damages the human society severely and it causes dangerous diseases to death. The human behaviour is also a reason for this environmental degradation. The fast moving of the world has brought out so many dangerous diseases and new challenging hazards in every one's life. Though heat is basic thing for every move in the life of human being, the aggressive and exited thoughts produce inauspicious omen and ill-health to the atmosphere which exterminates everyone in the society and around. The latest threat to the society is the usage of electrical and electronic goods which is inevitable and more over has become a part of our life. These domestic hazards are like known devils which no one knows how to escape from the clutches of these nuances of nuisance.

The latest threat in the field of E-good is mobile phones, i-pads, lap-tops etc. These items have become inevitable part of every elite. As per the latest statistics, the environment as well the users of these e-goods, get more mental worries and health related problems. Mobile phones and cell phones play a vital role in everyone's life irrespective of caste and creed. This up-coming threat is a deep worry to the environmentalists. In simple words, every house is a tenant of environment threats.

The Duty of Individual and Government

Individuals can help to avoid environment pollution by avoiding burning of coal, fossil fuels, plastic and rubber goods, minimize the interaction with the e-goods and doing plantation of trees.

From the poor to rich, everyone must be instructed about the environment degradation. The importance of Ozone layer must be taught among the people all over the world especially in the rural areas. The urban aristocrats must be insisted to follow the rules and regulations of the motor-act. The Government should implement Clean Air Act rule to reduce the mass pollution. Every industry must be brought under strict vigilance to follow the rules of the Government. Planting tree must be encouraged by the Government and non-governmental organizations. The water resources must be protected and hygienic environment should be created even to the last cadre of the society. Drainage system should be maintained clean in all the parts of the city. Public toilets may be maintained clean for the welfare of the society, especially for the sake of the down trodden community.

The View of the Skeptics

Each day passing brings yet new proof that we are now in front of a global emergency, a climate emergency that needs instant action to piercingly decrease carbon dioxide emissions worldwide in order to turn down the earth's rising temperatures and avoid any catastrophe. The global warming skeptics are of the view that the global warming is a good phenomenon and should not be stopped. There are various benefits of global warming according to them. According to the skeptics, the global warming will increase humidity in tropical deserts. Also the higher levels of carbon dioxide in the atmosphere trigger plant growth. As predicted, due to the global warming the sea levels will rise. But this can be readily adapted. Another argument of global warming skeptics is that earth has been warmer than today as seen in its history. The thought is that global warming is nothing to get afraid of because it just takes us back to a more natural set of environment of the past. Animals and plants appeared to do just fine in those eras of warm climate on the earth. According to few skeptics, the present chilly climate on the earth is an abnormality when judged over the geographical scale. Over geologic time, the earth's mean temperature is 22 degrees C, as compared to today's 15.5 degrees C.

Conclusion

Whatever may be the threat, environmental degradation paves way to global warming and this global warming is a threat to everyone living under the Sun. It is very urgent and utmost need of the hour to take necessary steps to stop global warming.

References

1. Articles from various Magazines.
2. Internet Sources.

11

Indian Global Warming and Climate Change in Agricultural Production

S. Gobi*
Dr. B. Muniyandi**

Introduction

Although no major impact has been observed on wheat production due to global warming in India in the recent past, the government has taken preventive steps to safeguard the principal crop from rising temperature. Data show there has been increasing trend since 2007-08 in wheat production, which alone contributes over 71 per cent of total food grain production of the country. Wheat production increased from 78.51 million tonnes in 2007-08 to 80.71 million tonnes in 2009-10 (as per 4th advance estimates, 2010), Studies have forecast adverse affect of global warming on wheat and other crops. Research findings of ICAR (Indian Council for Agricultural Research) on wheat crop has indicated that there is about 3 to 4 per cent decrease in grain yield with 1 degree Celsius rise in temperature during grain filling stage. Out of 28 million

* Ph, D., Research Scholar, Department of Economics, Bharathiar University, Coimbatore. Email: s.gopisrinivasan@gmail.com

** Professor and Head, Department of Economics, Bharathiar University, Coimbatore.

hectare area under wheat in India, about 9 million hectare in North Eastern plain zone, Central zone and peninsular zone is prone to terminal heat stress. Studies have revealed that the mean annual surface air temperature over India has risen by 0.56 degree Celsius during 1901-2009, which is above normal since 1990 over a base period of 1961-90. Although no adverse affect of global warming has been noticed on wheat in India so far, the government has taken some timely precautionary steps. Heat tolerant varieties like DBW 14, DBW 16, Raj 3765, Lok 1, GW 322 etc., have been popularised on larger scale under schemes like National Food Security Mission-wheat and Integrated Cereals Development Programme in Wheat. This is based on cropping systems aimed at increasing production and productivity of wheat, Thomas had said. In addition to this, crop advisories are issued to wheat growing farmers for adopting latest crop production/ protection technologies. Advisories are also issued for timely sowing, resource conservation technology including zero seed drill and irrigation at critical stages to mitigate the sudden rise in temperature. Besides, ICAR has also initiated networking projects for developing thermal and drought tolerant genotypes that are suitable for changing climatic scenario.

Global Warming India

India is a large country with all types of climates and different kinds of soil requiring different types of farming. Most of the agricultural land in India is dependent on rainfall for irrigation. While some parts of the country are drought prone, the other parts are prone to flooding. For many years, parts of the country have been struggling against drought and at the same time, agricultural lands in other parts of the country are submerged due to floods. In such a country, the effects of global warming will be extreme. India has about 15 Argo-climatic zones with different types of farming methods and crops. As most of the population is dependent on agriculture and two-thirds of the country waits for the monsoon rains to aid in agriculture, any change in the frequency of the rains will affect these areas critically.

Years of man's greed have paid the price, for the environment is changing and tomorrow's world may not be as we see it today. We will be gone, but our children will face the consequences. India, a developing nation, is ill equipped to deal with global warming effects such as drastic climate changes. The inertia in its government machinery will make it even more difficult to act on this issue. The signs are certain, as in the Himalayas, also known as the crown of India, the average temperatures are up by one degree Celsius and have lead to an increased melting of the glaciers. Most of the rivers feed off of the glaciers and the nation, in turn, is fed off of these rivers.

Global Warming and Climate Change

The signs of global warming are everywhere and every summer appears to be hotter than the last. Wells are running dry and the ground water has depleted. In April, all of India experienced the temperatures that are usually common in May. In Uttarakhand and Himanchal Pradesh, the states famous for their apples, the production has fallen due to temperature rise and less rain and snow. The apple belt has shifted 30 k.m., northward to higher altitudes from 9000 feet to 12,000 feet above sea level. In high altitude areas like Laddakh, with less agricultural possibilities, now it is possible to grow a larger variety of vegetables due to the increase in temperature. Houses in the foothills of the Himalayas have begun to install ceiling fans for the first time, as the average temperatures have increased. The increase in temperature has brought with them mosquitoes and house flies, which were uncommon until now. Malaria, which is found to be rare at a height of 1500 meters above sea level, is now more common in towns like Nainital, which is 2000 meters above sea level. Farmers all over India are switching over to crops requiring less water as the rains have become irregular. In many places, the farmers are planting the upland rice varieties that do not require stagnant water like the coastal varieties. Grapes are requiring a larger amount of water for irrigation and growth; this again is attributed to the climate change. As the winter rains have shifted to April in Himanchal Pradesh, they wash away the pollens of the apple flowers, thus contributing to a lower yield of the crop. Wheat production in India is decreasing every year due to the change in climate and other global warming effects. According to IARI, every 1°C increase in temperature reduces wheat production by 4-5 million tons. In high altitude areas like Leh, the tropical vegetables like bitter gourd, pumpkin, tomato, watermelon, and capsicum could not be grown locally and had to be imported from lower altitude areas in the past. It is now common to see farmers from these areas growing the same vegetables for personal as well as commercial use. In fact, the seas and the fisheries also have been affected by global warming as the Sardines are shifting from the Arabian Sea to the Bay of Bengal, traditionally not their normal habitat.

Social Effects of Climate Change in India

Global warming is affecting the livelihood of the people of the Himalayas, who for centuries were accustomed to farming in a particular way. As Himalayan farming is only dependent on the monsoon and the winter rains, this change has hit them hard. Now new crops and the methods to grow them have to be taught to the villagers and research based upon the local conditions and limitations must be done. As terraced farming has become more labour intensive and many times futile due to crop failures caused by global warming, many farmers are migrating to adjoining states and cities like New Delhi looking for employment. The crime rate has gone up and it is understandable, as loss of job opportunities have caused this. Vidharba region in the state of Maharashtra in news for the last few years because continuous suicides by farmers due to drought. As large areas are dependent of the rains for farming, the absent and irregular rains hit the farmers hard. As two-thirds of the population of India is dependent on monsoons for agriculture, the huge change in climate caused by global warming will affect them strongly. As the Himalayan glaciers are melting it will lead to a very thirsty India in the summer months. One research study has shown the Himalayas to be warming 5 to 6 times faster than the global average. An increase in temperatures coupled with the depletion of the ground water, will increase the diseases among the people.

Sustainable Development

The word sustainable development has very well known implications. It has both socio and economic content. It involves use of natural resources. It implies socio-economic growth rate in a compounded manner. It means to provide enough of what one needs in order to live or exists and grow on a sustainable basis. It also implies gradual socio-economic growth increase in size, quantity and quality. It also involves development of wealth of an area, people and society of a country. It is a long-term and eternal activity. It is a process whereby human beings try to shape and reshape the natural environment. This involves a patter of resource use that aims to meet the current human needs while preserving the environment so that need of the future generation can also be met comfortable and satisfaction. It implies a strategic solution for meeting the need of the present without compromising the ability of future generations to meet their own needs.

The process involves introduction/involvement and in economic activity by special initiative generally known as development programmes/schemes. Such programmes have three components: Economic agenda for inclusive growth, which aims to improve the economic status of majority of people with focus on poor families. Provision of basic social infrastructure and sufficient quality, road, water supply, education, credit services, power, irrigation etc. Utilisation of natural resources in a way that nature's equilibrium balance is not affected of its five important forces are the Sky (atmosphere), Sun, Earth, Water and Vegetation. These are also resources which sustain habitat. Over use of one or improper use of another affects balance and creates natural calamities which is now called as 'Global Warming'. The programme for sustainable development varies from country to country and from area-to-area and even from families to families. The development of an area or poor families is key to evolve such programmer and its implementation.

Agriculture

The only known-technology, which can absorb CO_2, is vegetation. The green leaves absorb CO_2 through process known as photosynthesis and release oxygen. We therefore feel there is need to inter act this important issue about role of agriculture vegetation and soil management to meet the impact of climate change and global warming. Agriculture has also major role to play in Sustainable Development. Majority of the poor people of the world apart from India depend for their livelihood on agriculture. The major impact on global warming which results into either delay in monsoon or heavy monsoon or flood is on small farmers who are wiped out for their income generating source for that year and pushed back below poverty line. On the other hand, there are un-cultivated, un-utilised land resources of wasteland, marshy land, fallow Agri land where vegetation can grow and provide employment. It can thus play very important role for mitigating climate change and its impact. With the global warming destined to go strong, India wheat output may be affected by the phenomenon; quantity-wise and quality-wise. According to him, global warming will affect crop cycles of wheat by lengthening them. Coupled with acute water shortage and temperature rise wheat output (as well as rice output) will be negatively affected in north-west India, reported Indian Express. Crops would be affected by diseases and pests as well. Also, climate change will have a negative impact on all four dimensions of food security-food availability, food accessibility, food utilisation, and food systems stability, reported Indian Express. Vector-borne diseases are likely to spread with mosquitoes shifting to new areas and many diseases thought to be eradicated resurrecting. Meanwhile, cold weather prevailing in parts of North India is promising for wheat cultivators, as the weather may support high wheat output this year, say reports from last week. The output is expected to match 2010 yields of 81 million tons of wheat. The acreage of wheat has also gone up by 8.95 lakh hectares to 291.36 lakh hectares. The pests are also restricted by cold weather. Punjab, Haryana, western Uttar Pradesh, Rajasthan and Madhya Pradesh are the prime wheat producing states in India and cold conditions have been prevailing in these States.

Table 11.1 show that the agriculture production-major commercial crops from 1999-2000 and 2009-10. Production of total oilseeds has increased from 20.71 tonnes in 1999-00 to 24.93 tones 2009-10. Total oilseeds highest production was 29.76 tones in 2007-08 and lowest production was 14.84 tonnes in 2002-03. The estimated compound growth rate was positive and it 4.41 per cent.

Production of coffee has increased from 292 tonnes in 1999-00 to 289.60 tonnes 2009-10. The highest production was 301.20 tonnes in 2000-01 and lowest production was 262 tonnes in 2002-03. The estimated compound growth rate was positive and it -0.82 per cent.

Production of cotton has increased from 11.53 tonnes in 1999-00 to 23.94 tonnes 2009-10. The highest production was 25.88 tonnes in 2007-08 and lowest production was 8.62 tonnes in 2002-03. The estimated compound growth rate was positive and it 11.66 per cent. Raw jute and Mesta has increased from 10.55 tonnes in 1999-00 to 11.29 tonnes 2009-10. The highest production was 11.68 tonnes in 2002-02 and lowest production was 10.27 tonnes in 2004-05. The estimated compound growth rate was positive and it 0.10 per cent. Sugarcane has increased from 299.32 tonnes in 1999-00 to 277.75 tonnes 2009-10. The highest production was 355.52 tonnes in 2006-07 and lowest production was 233.86 tonnes in 2003-04. The estimated compound growth rate was positive and it 0.51 per cent. Tea has increased from 836.86 tonnes in 1999-00 to 991.18 tonnes 2009-10. The highest production was 991.18 tonnes in 2009-10 and lowest production was 836.86 tones in 1999-00. The estimated compound growth rate was positive and it 2.01 per cent.

Table 11.1: Agricultural Production – Major Commercial Crops

(Million Tonnes)

Year	Oilseeds				Coffee	Cotton	Raw Jute and Mesta	Sugarcane	Tea	Tobacco
	Groundnut	Rapeseed and Mustard	Soyabean	Total						
1999-00	5.25	5.79	7.08	20.71	292.00	11.53	10.55	299.32	836.86	0.25
2000-01	6.41	4.19	5.28	18.44	301.20	9.52	10.56	295.96	848.43	0.34
2001-20	7.03	5.08	5.96	20.66	300.60	10.00	11.68	297.21	851.41	0.55
2002-03	4.12	3.88	4.66	14.84	275.30	8.62	11.28	287.38	845.97	0.49
2003-04	8.13	6.29	7.82	25.19	270.50	13.73	11.17	233.86	878.65	0.55
2004-05	6.77	7.59	6.88	24.35	275.50	16.43	10.27	237.09	906.84	0.55
2005-06	7.99	8.13	8.27	27.98	274.00	18.50	10.84	281.17	948.94	0.55
2006-07	4.86	7.44	8.85	24.29	288.00	22.63	11.27	355.52	973.07	0.52
2007-08	9.18	5.83	10.97	29.76	262.00	25.88	11.21	348.19	987.02	0.49
2008-09	7.17	7.20	9.91	27.72	262.30	22.28	10.37	285.03	972.77	–
2009-10	5.51	6.41	10.05	24.93	289.60	23.94	11.29	277.75	991.18	–
CGR	1.65	4.31	7.00	4.41	-0.82	11.66	0.10	0.51	2.01	10.504

Note: Data for 2009-10 are based on Advance Estimates.

Source: Ministry of Agriculture, Government of India.

Table 11.2 shows that the Area under Cultivation – Major Commercial Crops from 1999-2000 and 2009-10. Cultivation of total oilseeds has increased from 24.28 (MH) in 1999-00 to 26.22 tones 2009-10. Total oilseeds highest cultivation was 27.86 in 2005-06 and lowest cultivation was 21.49 in 2002-03. The estimated compound growth rate was positive and it 2.04 per cent. Sugarcane has increased from 4.22 in 1999-00 to 4.18 tonnes 2009-10. The highest cultivation was 5.15 in 2006-07 and lowest cultivation was 3.93 in 2002-03. The estimated compound growth rate was positive and it 0.72 per cent. Tea has increased from 0.49 in 1999-00 to 0.58 in 2009-10. The highest cultivation was 0.58 tonnes in 2009-10 and lowest cultivation was 0.49 in 2002-03. The estimated compound growth rate was positive and it 1.91 per cent. Coffee has increased from 0.31 in 1999-00 to 0.40 2009-10. The highest cultivation was 0.40 in 2009-10 and lowest production was 0.39 in 1999-00. The estimated compound growth rate was positive and it 2.96 per cent. Cotton has increased from 8.71 in 1999-00 to 10.28 2009-10. The highest cultivation was 10.28 in 2009-10 and lowest cultivation was 7.60 in 2003-04. The estimated compound growth rate was positive and it 1.65 per cent. Raw jute and Mesta has increased from 1.04 in 1999-00 to 0.91 in 2009-10. The highest Cultivation was 1.05 in 2001-02 and lowest Cultivation was 0.90 in 2005-06. The estimated compound growth rate was positive and it -1.57 per cent.

Table 11.3 shows that the Yield per Hectare – Major Commercial Crops from 1999-2000 and 2009-10. Yield per Hectare of total oilseeds has increased from 853 in 1999-00 to 969 in 2009-10. Total oilseeds highest Yield per Hectare was 1064 in 2003-04 and lowest Yield per Hectare was 810 in 2001-02. The estimated compound growth rate was positive and it 2.40 per cent. Sugarcane has increased from 70935 in 1999-00 to 65721 in 2009-10. The highest Yield per Hectare was 70935 in 1999-00 and lowest Yield per Hectare was 59380 in 2003-04. The estimated compound growth rate was positive and it -0.25 per cent. Tea has increased from 1707 in 1999-00 to 1711 in 2009-10. The highest Yield per Hectare was 1716 in 2006-07 and lowest Yield per Hectare was 1640 in 2002-03.

Table 11.2: Area under Cultivation – Major Commercial Crops

(Million Hectares)

Year	Oilseeds				Sugarcane	Tea	Coffee	Cotton (lint)	Raw Jute and Mesta	Tobacco
	Groundnut	Rapeseed and Mustard	Soyabean	Total						
1999-00	6.87	6.03	6.22	24.28	4.22	0.49	0.31	8.71	1.04	0.43
2000-01	6.56	4.48	6.42	22.77	4.32	0.50	0.31	8.53	1.02	0.26
2001-20	6.24	5.07	6.34	22.64	4.41	0.51	0.32	9.13	1.05	0.35
2002-03	5.94	4.54	6.11	21.49	4.52	0.52	0.33	7.67	1.04	0.33
2003-04	5.99	5.43	6.56	23.66	3.93	0.52	0.33	7.60	1.00	0.37
2004-05	6.64	7.32	7.57	27.52	3.66	0.52	0.33	8.79	0.92	0.37
2005-06	6.74	7.28	7.71	27.86	4.20	0.56	0.38	8.68	0.90	0.37
2006-07	5.62	6.79	8.33	26.51	5.15	0.57	0.38	9.14	0.94	0.37
2007-08	6.29	5.83	8.88	26.69	5.06	0.58	0.39	9.41	0.96	0.35
2008-09	6.64	6.30	9.51	27.56	4.42	0.58	0.39	9.41	0.90	–
2009-10	5.42	5.77	9.79	26.22	4.18	0.58	0.40	10.28	0.91	–
CGR	-1.00	2.45	5.25	2.04	0.72	1.91	2.96	1.65	-1.57	9.35

Note: Data for 2009-10 are based on Advance Estimates

Source: Ministry of Agriculture, Government of India.

Table 11.3: Yield per Hectare – Major Commercial Crops

(Yield per Hectare)

Year	Oilseeds				Sugarcane	Tea	Coffee	Cotton (lint)	Raw Jute and Mesta	Tobacco
	Groundnut	Rapeseed and Mustard	Soyabean	Total						
1999-00	766	960	1138	853	70935	1707	947	225	1836	1211
2000-01	977	935	822	810	68577	1682	959	190	1867	1318
2001-20	1127	1002	940	913	67370	1670	967	186	2007	1565
2002-03	694	854	762	691	63576	1640	839	191	1960	1506
2003-04	1357	1159	1193	1064	59380	1691	831	307	2008	1486
2004-05	1020	1038	908	885	64752	1739	826	318	2019	1498
2005-06	1187	1117	1073	1004	66928	1708	803	362	2173	1481
2006-07	866	1095	1063	916	69022	1716	840	421	2170	1409
2007-08	1459	1001	1235	1115	68877	1708	761	467	2101	1417
2008-09	1163	1143	1042	1006	64553	1679	748	403	2074	–
2009-10	993	1142	1076	969	65721	1711	826	396	2233	–
CGR	**2.84**	**1.95**	**1.88**	**2.40**	**-0.25**	**0.16**	**-2.18**	**9.86**	**1.67**	**- 44.45**

Note: Data for 2009-10 are based on Advance Estimates

Source: Ministry of Agriculture, Government of India

The estimated compound growth rate was positive and it 0.16 per cent. Coffee has increased from 947 in 1999-00 to 826 in 2009-10. The highest Yield per Hectare was 967 in 2001-02 and lowest Yield per Hectare was 748 in 2008-09. The estimated compound growth rate was positive and it -2.18 per cent. Cotton has increased from 2250 in 1999-00 to 396 in 2009-10. The highest Yield per Hectare was 467 in 2007-08 and lowest Yield per Hectare was 186 in 2001-02. The estimated compound growth rate was positive and it 9.86 per cent. Raw jute and Mesta has increased from 1836 in 1999-00 to 2233 in 2009-10. The highest Yield per Hectare was 2233 in 2009-10 and lowest Yield per Hectare was 1836 in 1999-00. The estimated compound growth rate was positive and it 1.67 per cent.

Conclusion

Agricultural production is very much dependent upon environmental variables and is also an important agent of environmental change. Hence it is critical to examine the possible consequences of global warming on agricultural sustainability and food security. Climate change will affect agriculture in different regions of the world in different proportions. Some factors that will play an important role are the degree of temperature increase, its geographic distribution, precipitation patterns (which will determine water supply to crops), radiation and other climate parameters. Hot and arid region countries are likely to face decrease in productivity and cold countries may start producing food. So there will be a shift in the place of production. The role of climate as a determinant of agriculture has long been recognised. It is only in the last decade, however, that the reciprocal effect has come to light: the role of agriculture as a potential contributor to climate change. Clearing forests for fields, burning crop residues, submerging land in rice paddies, raising large herds of cattle and other ruminants and fertilizing with nitrogen, all release greenhouse gases to the atmosphere.

More over with industrialisation, our food is now grown and processed in fewer locations, and it has to travel a long distance to reach the average consumer. Although this method of production is considered efficient and economically profitable for large agribusiness corporations, it is harmful to the environment, rural communities and consumers. A large amount of fossil fuel is used to transport foods through long distances. Combustion of these fuels releases harmful gases, particulate matter and other pollutants into the atmosphere, contributing to global climate change. Food miles can be reduced through localisation of food. We could consume local foods which are raised nearby, are fresh and undergo minimal processing. This will also help small farmers and entrepreneurs to gain self-sufficiency in food production and distribution. Modern commercialised agricultural practices are affecting the world's scarce, non-renewable resources. Genetic modification of crops is posing a high risk.

References

1. http://www.gcrio.org/Consequences/summer95/agriculture.html
2. Pierre Crosson 1997 Impacts of Climate Change on Agriculture *Climate Issues Brief* No. 4 June 1997.
3. Ethan Ligon and Elizabeth Sadoulet (2008), Estimating the Effects of Aggregate Agricultural Growth in the Distribution of Expenditures. Background Paper for the World Development Report 2008, 2007.
4. Seema Jayachandran (2006), Selling Labour Low: Wage Responses to Productivity Shocks in Developing Countries. *Journal of Political Economy*, 114(3):538.575, 2006.
5. William R. Cline (1992), The Economics of Global Warming. Peterson Institute for International Economics, 1992.
6. Balakrishnan Pulapre, Ramesh Golait, Pankaj Kumar (2008), Agriculture Growth in India Since 1991, Study No. 27, Department of Economic Analysis and Policy, RBI, Mumbai.
7. Vijay Paul Sharma (2007), India's Agrarian Crisis and Smallholder Producers' Participation in New Farm Supply Chain Initiatives: A Case Study of Contract Farming, W.P. No. 2007-08-01, Indian Institute of Management, Ahmedabad.
8. Ramasamy C. (2004), "Constraints to Growth in Indian Agriculture: Needed Technology, Resource Management and Trade Strategies", *Indian Journal of Agriculture Economics*, Vol. 59 (1), pp. 1-41.

12

Global Warming and Its Effects on Human Health

V. L. Lavanya

> *"The earth is the only place in the universe where there is life. Its continued survival now rests in our hands".*
>
> **— David Attenborough**

Global warming has captured the centre stage of the worldwide attention and has inspired more debates and action at every level than any other environmental issue in history. Global warming is now recognised as threat to humanity but many infectious organisms will emerge as beneficiaries, especially the parasites that are already responsible for a major part of the disease burden faced by the poor in developing countries. Global warming is bound to affect the basic requirements for maintaining health – clean air and water, sufficient food, adequate shelter, and freedom from disease As the concentration of the heat absorbent greenhouse gases increases, more and more heat becomes trapped in the atmosphere and less heat escapes back into space. This increase in the trapped heat raises the surface temperature of

Ph.D Research Scholar, Department of Economics, Avinashilingam Deemed University for Women, Coimbatore.

the earth and changes the climate. This is called global warming. Global warming not only poses a significant threat to the earth's ecology, but also unleashes an unprecedented health risks due to heat waves, spread of infectious diseases, disasters and malnutrition. India is a large developing country of sub-continental proportions home to 1.1 billion people or 17 per cent of the world's population. A large proportion of this population continues to live in rural areas and depends heavily on climate-sensitive sectors such as agriculture, fisheries and forestry for its livelihood. With rapid economic growth, however, the demand for goods, services and energy has soared and large shortfalls are emerging.

Global Warming in India

In India, global warming has caused tremendous changes in the weather patterns across different parts of the country. The consequences will be irreparable and it will affect the environment, economy and social welfare of a particular region or country. The annual monsoon season will lead to severe droughts and floods in various parts of India. So, India is on the fast track of becoming a global economy and on the other hand industrialisation and urbanisation leads to more greenhouse gas emissions which in turn cause climate change mainly impacting the monsoon rains. India emits 1.7 billion tonnes of greenhouse gases each year, as of 2007. Despite a growing economy, emissions intensity (GHGs per unit of GDP) has dropped and is 20 per cent lower than the global average. Future emissions are set to grow rapidly, owing to high economic growth rates and carbon-intensive development. With current development patterns and business – as usual growth, India could be responsible for up to 6 billion tonnes of GHG emissions by 2030 and lock-in carbon-intensive practices in all areas of growth (industry, buildings, transport, and power). In the mid-term, the Indian government has pledged to cut its carbon intensity by 20 to 25 per cent below 2005 levels by 2020.

Effects of Global Warming on Human Health

India is experiencing a stage where non-communicable diseases and lifestyle related diseases are showing a rising trend while communicable diseases continue to cause morbidity and mortality with emergence of new pathogens posing a serious challenge. Vector borne diseases especially dengue infection, which was earlier restricted to urban areas only, is now being widely reported from rural areas as well. It has spread to new areas of the country as well. Chikungunya has been widely reported last year and trends of water borne diseases like acute diarrhoea diseases, cholera and enteric fever do not show much change in incidence over last 10 years but a definitive conclusion cannot be made in view of weaknesses in the disease surveillance system. Increase in temperature correlate with increased populations of some micro organisms that cause waterborne diseases, such as Vibrio cholera bacterium, which causes Cholera. The increase of Chloro Fluoro Carbons in the atmosphere, leading to global warming will increase UV radiation in the atmosphere, affecting the immune systems and leading to infectious diseases. Other minor effects are increased incidence of skin disorders, such as prickly heat and fungal skin disorders such as ringworm and athlete's foot as a result of increased temperature and humidity.

Global warming not only poses a significant threat to the earth's ecology, but also unleashes an unprecedented health risks due to heat waves, spread of infectious diseases, disasters and malnutrition. As per WHO estimate, global warming currently contributes to more than 1.5 lakh deaths 11 and more than 50 lakh illnesses every year. 1150 million environmental refugees, displaced by floods, droughts and rising sea levels are expected by 2010 and it may double by 2030. Experts apprehend that global warming will kill billions in this century.

Effect of Hot Climate

- There will be an increased intensity, duration and frequency of heat waves around the world.
- The sick and the elderly persons are most vulnerable, for their decreased ability to increase cardiac output and decreased sweat function for cooling of body. Technological

adaptations, *e.g.*, installation of air-conditioners and construction of heat minimizing houses will happen quickly among the rich.

- In the developed nations it will affect the poor more than the rich and in the developing world it will affect the nations least able to respond to these threats and stresses. Overall, global warming has more and disproportionate effect on the under developed countries and on the poorer segments of the society. There is increased risk of bush fire or forest fire, which can kill people.

Effect of Floods

- There are health effects secondary to flooding, such as contaminated water supplies and breakdown in sewerage and garbage services, leading to spread of the whole range of water borne diseases, food borne diseases and other infectious diseases. Contamination of swimming water also invites some health hazards.
- Water logging hampers food distribution with natural consequences on health.

Effect of Increasing Air Pollution

- Increasing air pollution from the continued burning of fossil fuels will cause higher rates of respiratory and cardiovascular diseases.
- With warming, there will be an increase in pollens, mold spores and release of large quantities of particulate matters, aggravating the hazards of asthma.
- Increased ground level ozone damages lung tissue, induces and increases asthma and invites many other cardio-respiratory diseases.
- Depletion of stratospheric ozone allows more and more UV-rays to enter into the atmosphere and thus increases the incidence of malignancies.

Effect of Disasters

- There will be a sharp rise in the storms, heavy rainfall, sea-water flood, draughts, forest-fire, earthquakes, tsunami and volcanoes.

- Hospitals, health services, ambulances, fire services, electricity, food and water supply, transport and all sorts of communications become ineffective altogether, after the disaster, with a massive impact on health and life.
- These disasters invariably increase the psychological stress, depression, agony and a feeling of isolation among people affected by natural disasters.

Table 12.1: Global Warming and Health Impacts

Global Warming Effects on	Adverse Health Impacts
Floods, storms	Deaths, injuries, infectious disease outbreaks, mental health impacts on affected communities.
Heat waves	Deaths, hospitalisations, emergency department visits, and heat-related illnesses.
Air pollution	Increased concentrations of ground-level ozone smog and fine particulate matter, increasing premature mortality and hospitalisations.
Airborne allergen Production	Increased allergic illnesses (hay fever, asthma) due to longer pollen season and increases in the amount of pollen produced.
Insect-borne Infections	Infections carried by mosquitoes, ticks, and other insects can spread into new areas.
Water-borne Infections	Risk of cholera could be increased as coastland estuarine waters warm; extreme rainfall events are associated with increased risks of *Cryptosporidium* outbreaks.
Water and food Supplies	More frequent drought, reduced drinking water supplies and crop yields, increasing world food insecurity; declining fisheries can contribute to protein shortages; increased risks of food-borne Illnesses.
Sea-level rise	Contamination of coastal soils and drinking water supplies; increasing storm surges and floods; large numbers of displaced people.

Source: Global Warming and Infectious Diseases, World Health Organization.

Table 13.1 depicts that climate and weather have a powerful impact on human life and health. Certain health outcomes associated with the prevailing environmental conditions include illnesses and death associated with temperatures extremes, storms and other heavy precipitation events, air pollution, water contamination and diseases carried by vectors. As a result of the potential consequences of these stresses acting individually or in combination it is possible that projected climate change will have measurable impacts on health.

Protection of health from global warming has to be a part of a basic, preventive approach to public health. There is a close link between local climate and the occurrence or severity of some diseases and other threats to human health. It is estimated that climate change contributes to 150,000 deaths and 5 million illnesses each year, WHO estimates that a quarter of the world's disease burden is due to the contamination of air, water, soil and food. In the last quarter of the 20th century, the average atmospheric temperature rose by about 1 degree Fahrenheit. By 2000, that increase was responsible for the annual loss of about 160,000 lives and the loss of 5.5 million years of healthy life, according to estimates by the WHO. The toll is expected to double to about 300,000 lives and 11 million years of healthy life by 2020. Most of the increased burden of death and disease were from malnutrition, diarrhoea, malaria, heat waves, and floods. But those diseases will play a minor role, at best, in many regions that nevertheless will feel the effects of global warming.

Conclusion

Global warming has various effects, ranging from economical, environmental as well as the health life of human beings. The global warming effect on human health suspected will occur more in developing countries and affect 88 per cent of the children. Poor people and the poor nations are the worst sufferers. The results affecting our health are killer heat waves, devastating droughts, ocean expansion, heavy rainfall, coastal flood, fierce storms, massive spread of the whole range of mosquito-borne diseases like malaria, dengue, Chikungunya, encephalitis and yellow fever, along with the effects of flood, spread of water borne diseases like cholera, effects of droughts, malnutrition, water scarcity, increasing air pollution and disasters. Proactive health adaptation strategies are needed to protect the world's most vulnerable people from the effects of global warming. Policy-makers will need to work to strengthen the health-care systems, along with water and wastewater systems. In order to better address some of the predicted changes taking place in India more emphasis may be required on the following policies:

- Health and welfare, provision of drinking water and sanitation, accessibility of health centres with malaria treatment facilities and educating people about malaria and other climate related diseases.
- Policies on urban planning, provision of funding for low income communities with poor sheltering and high exposure/risk to heat and cold waves.

References

1. Majra J.P and Gur. A, (2009), "In Climate change and health: Why should Indian be Concerned?", *Indian Journal of Occupational and Environmental Medicine*, April, Volume 13, Issue 1, pp. 11-16.
2. Ahern .M.J and Matthias F. (2005), "Global Health Impacts of Floods" Epidemiological Evidence, *Epidemiological Reviews*, Volume 27, pp. 36-45.
3. Jonathan Patz *et al.*, (2008), "Health Impact Assessment of Global Climate Change: Expanding on Comparative Risk Assessment Approaches for Policy Making", *The Annual Review of Public Health,* Vol. 29, pp. 27-39.
4. Ebi K.L, Smith J, Burton I and Scheraga JS (2006), "Some Lessons Learned from Public Health on the Process of Adaptation", Mitigation and Adaptation Strategies for Global Change, Vol. 11, pp. 607-620.
5. Epstein, Paul R., Andrew Haines, and Anthony J. McMichael. (2000), Global Warming and Health". *Canadian Medical Association Journal*, pp. 729-734.

13

Global Warming and the Initiatives of Environmental Awareness

Dr. P. Muthukumar

Life on earth and the life of earth are getting jeopardized because of global warming. Human beings life closer to nature for millions of years saved him and the earth. The inventions and innovations of human brain had drained all the potential strength of the earth by releasing extraordinary emissions of fumes such as carbon dioxide, nuclear waste, industrial pollution and automobile fossil fuel. The steps of man on earth hardly harmed any life but the adventure of his mind harmed all living beings in total.

Human beings desire for cosmetic life had brought more danger to the earth than the natural disaster so far. Since the day man had altered course of nature, the nature inurn started altering the course of his life. What was not developed for thousands of years were developed technically in these two hundred years. The last two hundred years of scientific advancement brought more changes than the changes brought by past two hundred years. Exploration of soil had exposed the earth to various dangerous radiations such as nuclear and

Associate Professor, Department of Political Science, Presidency College, Chennai.

uranium substances. And extraordinary mining for survival of human life are actually suffocating the life itself.

Modernisation and urbanisation process had triggered the desire of human needs, forcing them to contest against nature. The net result of such contest against nature is forcing the scientific community to discuss a new planet for the human dwellings. The warmth of globe is generating heat amidst populated earth. The loss of wild animals and birds and the endangered species caged in zoos is an indicator for human extinction. Someday humans may also be caged as an endangered species.

Global warming in an alarming proportion is disturbing our very existence. However it is sad to note that the majority of human beings are not aware of their journey towards extinction. The depletion of ozone layer and the entry of unfiltered ultraviolet rays into earth consistently for years would naturally affect the nature of earth. The pollution level in the atmosphere is beyond compromises. The paper explore the impact of climate change, causes of ozone depletion, pollution of world oceans, impact of acid rain, loss of tropical forest, soil erosion and the awareness initiatives on environment.

Climate Change

Atmospheric pollution is on a global scale. Our planet is under the suffocation of excessive carbon dioxide emission. The increased concentration of carbon dioxide in the atmosphere are due to the burning of fossil fuel, which in turn causes climate change. There are more than 70,000 chemicals are used and released into the environment without knowing the long-term effect of the chemicals to the environment.[1]

Ozone Layer

Ozone layer a life sustaining jacket of earth lost the strength to withstand the levels of pollution and started leaving way for ultraviolet radiation of sun. The entry of unfiltered sun rays adds woes to the already damaged earth environment. The depletion of ozone layer is an indicator of danger for the sustenance of living beings on earth.

Acid Rain

Acid rain is an international problem. The aim of industrial places all over the world push pollution high into the air, dispersing the pollutants of dangerous substance through rain.[2]

Loss of Tropical Forests

Deforestation also influences local, regional and possibly even global climatic conditions by altering hydrological regions, reducing vegetation cover and causing more heat and light to be reflected back to the atmosphere (the albedo effect), and through accelerated burning of the forest biomass, which contributes to carbon dioxide build-up in the atmosphere and the global warming trend. The economic, social and political implications of possible regional and global climate changes have only begun to be assessed. Tropical forests are vanishing at alarming rate and it needs community based forestry scheme to protect the environment.[3]

Soil Loss

Land degradation is a recent phenomenon primarily related to the historical and political ramifications of the latter half of the 19th century and early part of the 20th century.[4] Almost every environmental concern connects clearly with we importance of soil. Soil acts as a reservoir for water and other inorganic substances cycling through the eco-system. It provides habitat for many of the different population or decomposer organisms that control the rate and capacity of nutrient recycling. The importance of soil to agriculture can hardly be over emphasized. Agriculture provides, about 44 per cent of the poorest countries gross domestic product and 83 per cent of their employment. Growing more food, building irrigation projects, conserving nature and precious wildlife and other needs must depend on proper soil management. The wide-ranging importance of soil confirms that soil management must consequently be many-sided. The broad range of natural and man-made stress that causes the two type of soil damage: physical displacement and alterations in solid structure and composition.[5]

Public Awareness

Public awareness can be brought about by environmental education for the individuals and social groups. Real life environmental problems can be sorted out by developing attitude, skill and abilities. The mass media such as radio, television, news papers, magazines, posters, street plays, door to door campaigning and educational institutions can play a major sole in this regard. UNESCO (1975) laid down a few objectives and guiding principles for developing environmental awareness at all levels in both formal and non-formal setting.

Objectives

Attitude

To help social groups and individuals acquires a set of values and feelings of concern for the environment and the motivation for actively participating in environment protection.[6]

Awareness

To help social groups and individuals acquires awareness of sensitivity to the total environment and its allied problems.

Evaluation Ability

To help individuals and social groups evaluate environmental measures and education programmes in terms of ecological, economic, social, aesthetic and educational factors.

Knowledge

To help social groups and individuals gains a variety of experiences and acquire a basic understanding of the environment and its' associated problems.

Participation

To provide social groups and individuals with an opportunity to be actively involved at all levels in working towards the resolution of environmental problems.

Skill

To help social groups and individuals acquires skills for identifying and solving environmental problems. The environmental laws also need a thorough updating and revision. In fact this has to be a regular activity so that laws are able to meet the newer environmental challenges and insulate the country from future environmental damage. Straight laws should come into force particularly in the sensitive areas.[7]

Conclusion

Think globally and Act Locally has become the main slogan of Global environmental awareness. Our globe is becoming warm day-by-day. We humans are exploring our environment and exposing our self to Global disasters. Disasters by nature occurred for ages were managed by earth for millions of years. But the human intellectual advancement and his invention and innovation of technologies and their application contesting nature brings the human survival a huge task. Natural nuclear fusion energy from the sun gave earth so far the rejuvenated health. The advent of nuclear energy fused by humans had struck the clock of pandemonium. Though nuclear power is good for constructive purpose, it is mostly used as an offensive arsenal by all the developing and developed countries.

In a global completion every nation is involved in outsmarting other nations in some form or other. Fiscal centric approach for nation's progress affects nations understanding of environment. And the inclusive growth of social community's world is the need of the hour. Advancing social forestry scheme in a global scale would bring lot of change in the standards of environmental understanding.

Whatever is lost is lost. But if we could not retrieve what is lost we could at least revive what is lost, if there is community effort globally with the commitment for the sustainable development.

References

1. Ministerial Declaration on Climate Change and Sustainable Development, New Delhi, 23 Oct. 1 Nov. 2002.
2. The Colombia Encyclopedia, Sixth Edition, Colombia University Press, 2004.

3. Stone .D. Roger and Claudia D Andrea., Tropical Forest and the Human Spirit, Journey to the Brink of Hope, University of California Press, 2005.

4. Khusoo. T.N. and Tejwani, T.G., Cambridge University Press, 1993.

5. Gurjar Ramkumar and Mathur Shichi., Environmental Studies. Ritu Publication, Jaipur, 2005.

6. Das Gupta, Debabrata, Environmental Studies and Education, Agrobios, Jodhpur, 2008.

7. Social Issues and Environment AITBS Publishers, New Delhi, 2005.

14

Women's Role in a Warming World

T. N. Geetha

Introduction

Global warming is not a disease; it is an atmospheric phenomenon, generally considered to be caused by humans. All of us in the world have a responsibility to end up with this planet as a habitable place. *Who can reduce global warming emissions? We can together*. Our individual efforts are important, but the biggest impact on climate change will come from large-scale changes well-reasoned international policies; thoughtful and systematic efforts to reduce polluting fossil fuel energy sources and unsound land use practices; and steady progress towards a green, sustainable future.

Global warming has emerged as one of the most important contentious international environmental issue. International efforts are ongoing to address this issue and in every summit this issue is being discussed. In the recently concluded G-8 summit the issue of global warming catches the attention of both the developed and developing countries. The earth is

Assistant Professor, PG Department of Economics, Government Arts College (Autonomous), Salem - 7. E-mail: Geethakumar@gmail.com getting warmer day-by-day. The burning of fossil fuels and other greenhouse gases is causing.

- Arctic ice cap melting.
- Rising sea levels.
- Changed rainfall patterns.
- Increased frequency and intensity of weather extremes like; floods, droughts, killer heat waves, wildfires, and hurricanes and cyclones.
- A plague of infectious diseases.
- Water scarcity.
- Agricultural disruption and loss of arable land.
- As many as one-third of plant and animal species extinct by 2050.
- Increasing disease.
- Displacement and economic losses from natural calamities like hurricanes.
- Reductions in the ozone layer.

Energy is a Human Right

The Solar Electric Light Fund (SELF) is a cutting-edge, independent not-for-profit organization that designs and implements sustainable energy solutions for enhancements in health, education, agriculture and economic growth in the developing world. SELF works to deliver solar power and wireless communications to rural villages in Africa, Asia, and Latin America. SELF facilitates a new generation of 'whole village' solar electrification projects to power, water pumping and purification, drip irrigation, health clinics (including vaccine refrigeration), schools, household community lighting, and income-generating micro-enterprises that can be scaled up through the private sector or through public sector partnerships.

Ay form of power generation which decreases the call on the world's natural resources, while reducing emissions, will have a long-term benefit. The traditional ways of producing power has a negative effect on the environment.

Solar power, being totally renewable, sustainable and without emissions will certainly help slow down global warming and its negative effects. One of the key ways that solar power will help the environment by providing an alternative for major electricity sources. While using 100 per cent solar power might not always be a viable alternative to conventionally produced electricity, it will certainly work as a back up and support. This will decrease our dependency on power produced by traditional methods. Working with government, industry and non-governmental organization partners, SELF has facilitated solar electricity projects in more than 20 countries.

How and Why Renewable Energy is Important for Women?

Women already have a track record of functioning as effective entrepreneurs. There are many visibly successful organizations and networks like Gramin Shakti, SEWA, TIDE, AIWC and SELCO) apart from a large and or organizations in South Asia, Africa etc. The challenge is to involve more women and transform them into energy entrepreneurs. The Gramin bank which provides small credits to women entrepreneurs in Bangladesh who are already marketing PV systems and operate cell phone through solar energy.

Credit is a critical constraint for women, whether as housewives or as entrepreneurs. Most banks require that borrowers be wage earners or property owners with acceptable collateral, condition that women often cannot meet. Limited education, complicated loan procedure and long distances to the bank further constraints women's access to credit. Lack of access to credit, is thus, a major constraint on women's purchase of renewable energy technologies.

The rural energy departments of All India Women's Conference (AIWC), Integrated Sustainable Energy and Ecological Development Association (INSEDA), and International Network for Sustainable Energy (INFORSE) all are striving to bring women and energy into the main stream.

The various domestic technologies available in India which directly benefit women, are:

1. Improved Cook Stoves.
2. Biogas.
3. Solar thermal devices: Box type solar cookers, parabolic cookers and solar storage cookers.
4. Solar water heater and Purifier.
5. Vermi Composting and nursery raising using biogas slurry.
6. Solar PV systems – solar lanterns, charging station, home light systems etc.

Current Status in the Field of Renewable Energy in India

As energy consumers and beneficiaries, women have contributed to design household's energy technologies and projects. As micro-entrepreneurs, women have used renewable energy to increase profits and efficiency in their informal sector enterprises and have proven themselves capable of operating and also constructing renewable energy technologies on their own, when provided with appropriate training and support. Women may be effective renewable energy entrepreneur, due to their experience as users of energy in households and their own enterprises; in some countries including India, women are already marketing solar home systems successfully.

As extension workers and caretakers, women have been effective in operation and maintenance roles of biogas, hydro electric and solar installations. As leaders, networkers and lobbyists women have successfully influenced energy policy decisions at the local, national and international levels. Women do not necessarily help to build, operate or maintain renewable energy installations alone, more important is that women have a role in determining the use and benefits of the projects and in managing these arrangements and they receive and control benefits. Women can save the environment and earn money for themselves and can earn carbon credit for the country.

One Carbon credit is equal to one ton of carbon dioxide avoided. Even small plants like bio-gas or improved Chullas could be 'bundled' and the organization could get carbon credit through registering with UN.

Solar Energy does Actually Prevent Global Warming

Solar energy produces electricity without going through the process of burning fossil fuels which is the most common reason for global warming. Furthermore, renewable energy can also provide energy to refrigerate medicine and sterilize medical equipment in rural areas where the access to electricity is difficult. It can also provide power for supplying fresh water and sewerage services needed to reduce infectious disease .Not only does it generate electricity, it also heats.

Water, purifies air, used for cooking, and tells time, so all these everyday actions can be done without burning any fossil fuels. Millions of people use only traditional energy as biomass-wood, residues and dung, for cooking and heating. The constant use of this type of energy exposed them to indoor particulate and carbon monoxide concentrations considered in many times higher than World Health Organization (WTO) standards. Traditional stoves using dung and charcoal emit large amounts of carbon monoxide and other noxious gases. Women and children suffer most, because they are exposed for the longest periods of time. Acute respiratory illnesses affect as much as 6 per cent of the world population. The WHO estimates that 2.5 million women and young children in developing countries die prematurely each year from breathing the fumes from indoor biomass stoves. Renewable energy can contribute to improve this situation by avoiding the exposure to indoor pollutants.

Women's Role in the Clean Energy Economy

The increase of temperature as a consequence of global warming has contributed to the loss of snow peaks, the increase of plagues and the change of agricultural cycles, affecting not only the regular practices of people but also the social and individual relationships that women and men have with their territories and natural resources that are necessary for their physical and cultural survival. Global warming generates not only changes in nature but also changes in the social dynamics increasing conflicts and social problems.

Furthermore, national and international local responses from organizations, institutions and individuals, have usually been given to men; showing that in this sense the gender perspective has not been totally considered. On the other hand, the measures to control global warming have been focused on compromises and agreements related to the control of green house effect gases, putting aside transformation processes related to daily activities like alimentary sovereignty and water management within others. This situation is not very different within indigenous women that need to discuss such a problem and propose strategies that respond to their relationships with their territories and resources and to the effects of their practices to mitigate global warming.

Globally gender-sensitive climate change adaptation and mitigation programmes show measurable results, Women's full participation in decision-making will save lives, protect fragile natural resources, reduce greenhouse gases and build resilience for current and future generations. Mechanisms or financing for disaster prevention, adaptation and mitigation will remain insufficient unless they integrate women's full participation-voices and hands – in design, decision-making and implementation.

Climate Change is not Gender Neutral

- Climate change affects women differently and more severely. It is the poor women who are more vulnerable and will bear the adaptation burden. This is because men and women have different roles and women by social defaults face discrimination in various forms. This also brings down the capacity of women to adapt.
- It is estimated that $125 billion was invested on renewable energy technology in 2006 to address climate change. Women have proven themselves capable of operating and also constructing renewable energy.

- Women's role in recycling and waste management within the households includes variety of opportunities to make women more important agent in resource conservation. Women should participate in all dialogue on the generation of solutions for disaster risk management and conflict prevention.

Engaging Women on Adaptation Strategies

Women in developing countries have an intimate knowledge of the social and natural systems of global warming affects. Women and girls are responsible for gathering cook stove fuel and producing 60 per cent to 80 per cent of the food in developing countries. According to the United Nations, women in Sub-Saharan Africa spend 40 billion hours a year collecting water. They can therefore provide valuable insight when it comes to formulating adaptation policies and implementing projects as fuel and water become scarce and agricultural yields shrink.

The first step to make women to participate in adaptation is recognising their values in International climate negotiations and supporting advocacy group work. Next is finding concrete ways to integrate women into the planning, development, and execution of climate adaptation strategies. Climate change and environmental policies must be intrinsically linked with gender, as women are often the first to be affected by our changing environment. Studies showed that while women are responsible for managing household resources, they typically don't have a say in the use and management of environmental resources integral to their households and communities. Governments and other stakeholders should ensure gender equality at the fore front of climate change initiatives, according to the Women's Environment and Development Organization (WEDO).

Climate adaptation strategy literature is minimal, but observers often turn to experience with disaster risk reduction to craft informed approaches. The disaster risk reduction community is also giving gender issues more consideration, which involves evaluating regional, national, and local response systems through a gender lens, collecting supplemental data, and ensuring women have equal access to early warning systems and the resources for preparedness and disaster assistance. Further, these techniques are made much more possible and effective with targeted financing, which is why as some argue that part of adaptation funding should be set aside for gender-specific training, community workshops, and disaster plans.

Absence of Women in Global Environment Policy

U.N. Human Rights Council states that the adverse effects caused by global warming will be more heavily felt by vulnerable populations, such as women. Practically all of the Millennium Development Goals in one way or another to questions that affect women education, health, maternity, poverty, infant mortality... and in all of these aspects, women are present, suffering the negative consequences or providing solutions.

But more important is the fact that this absence of participation by women acts in detriment of their ability to help fight climate change, while recognition of the role played by women would support their formal training, as well as their possibilities of contributing solutions to climate problems. It is recommended that specific measures on training for women should be given priority at the national and international levels in the framework of climate change policy, in order to strengthen the capacities that women already have with respect to the sustainable use and conservation of natural resources like water, energy sources, and forests.

India has 400 million people who are not even connected to the physical infrastructure of energy supply networks, an equal number who are served for less than 20 per cent of their time and the balance who pay energy prices that are comparable with most developed countries even without adjusting for purchasing power parity! About 90 per cent of India's rural population still uses biomass fuels for cooking.

Fighting Climate Change and Involving Women

The Human Development Report made the following recommendations:

- Develop a multilateral framework for avoiding dangerous climate change under the post – 2012 Kyoto Protocol.
- Put in place policies for sustainable carbon budgeting – the agenda for mitigation.
- Strengthen the framework for international co-operation.
- Put climate change adaptation at the centre of post – 2012 Kyoto framework and international partnerships for poverty reduction.

While these recommendations are important for fighting climate change, a gender dimension to these policies should be considered. WEDO recommended that governments ensure that women have access to participate in decisions related to climate change and that gender equality is incorporated in climate change initiatives, international and development agencies state that the effects of climate change will vary among different regions of the world, among different occupations, income groups, age groups and generations, and also between women and men. Therefore, they argue, it is vital that these different interests are represented in efforts to combat the effects of climate change.

Other Green Power Alternatives

If solar power isn't for you, then perhaps consider wind or water generated power. The locust is an excellent example of a wind farm providing power to over 6,500 homes. There are an increasing number of alternative options available for every one. They are severely affected by climate change yet under represented Renewable energy projects in many developing countries have demonstrated that renewable energy can directly contribute to poverty alleviation by providing the energy needed for creating businesses and employment. Renewable energy technologies can also make indirect contributions to alleviating poverty by providing energy for cooking, heating, and lighting.

Women are likely to be hit harder by climate change than men due their social roles and the simple fact that a majority – as much as 70 per cent – of the world's poor are women. As a result, they are much more devastated by natural disasters than men. Women are 14 times more likely than men to die in a natural disaster such as a tsunami. Experts predict climate change will only exacerbate such inequities.

But over the last few years the increasing portfolios of climate solutions include women's involvement. Observers realise that women need to be protected, engaged, and empowered for climate solutions. They also see that a vulnerable segment of the population is in fact one with mass potential to bring positive change. Women are a largely untapped resource that we must use to effectively and justly combat climate change. They need to be harnessed to prepare communities for global warming's effects, particularly in developing countries where warming will have the most severe consequences.

Progress in the UNFCCC

U.N. officials, United Nations Framework Convention on Climate Change (UNFCCC) country delegates, and non-governmental organizations are beginning to integrate gender into their discourse and policy pushes. A handful of NGOs have more publicly championed gender justice such as the international antipoverty organization care and the Women's Environment and Development Organization (WEDO). They held side events at the Copenhagen climate change conference last year on this very issue, and groups like climate wise women have since taken their message on the road. NGOs maintained pressure to include gender-sensitive language in the final text, and several governments were on board. Finland, Ecuador, Guatemala, Costa Rica, Bolivia, Iceland, Norway, the European Union, and several African countries supported gender – based language going into Copenhagen.

Groups like WEDO and Gender CC continue to push the United Nations to involve women at high-level climate negotiations. They note that at Copenhagen 30 per cent of the country delegates were women. On the one hand, this was the peak for women's engagement, but on the other hand it does not mirror reality.

Going Forward

Renewable energy can be particularly suitable for developing countries. In rural and remote areas, transmission and distribution of energy generated from fossil fuels can be difficult and expensive. Producing renewable energy locally can offer a viable alternative. Interest in renewable energies has increased in recent years due to environmental concerns about global warming and air pollution reduced costs of renewable energy technologies, and improved efficiency and reliability. Many recent trends reflect the importance of developing countries in advancing renewable energy. Collectively, developing countries have more than half of global renewable power capacity. China and India are rapidly expanding markets for renewable energy in the world. This might in the long run bring down the gender inequalities exacerbated by climate change in the World.

Conclusion

Economic development and concerns for the environment go hand in hand. If our consideration is only for economic development disregarding environment, definitely a day will come we have to repent and our future generations will suffer the devastating effects of the climatic alterations. On the other hand, to protect the climate and environment we cannot go back to the Stone Age. We are living in a globalised world now, with more developed technologies and faster means of communications.

We need economic development and at the same time we have to address the issues of preserving the environment and protecting the climate. To do both is possible through the use of alternative clean fuel and efficient energy saving technologies by including women as forerunners for such a change. The nexus between climate change and gender equality needs to be intensified, so that the capacity of the national and local institutions can be strengthened in terms of resilience to climate change by involving wide range of stakeholders.

References

1. Jyoti Parikh, Gender and Climate Change – Analysis, Policy and Action, www.undp.org,2008.
2. Lorena Aguilar, Women and Climate Change – Vulnerabilities and Adaptation, State of the World 2009, World Watch Institute, Washington DC, 2009.
3. http://www.wedo.org/files/climatechangeorange2ebook.pdf,2007.
4. Government of India (2008) National Action Plan on Climate Change, Prime Minister's Council on Climate Change New Delhi.
5. Key Note Address by Mrs. Harlem on Levers of Global Security Examining How A Changing Climate Impacts Women, 2007.

15

Impact of Global Warming in Economic Development

A. Senthil Kumar

"Environment does not belong to man
Man belongs to Environment"

Environment means surroundings. It is a system in which various living beings like animals including man, birds, insects, rodents, micro-organisms like algae, fungi, protozoa and non-living beings like the soil, the water, the air etc., are interrelated in a life sustaining. It is a complex web in which man is only a small tiny creature. Man lives in two environments, One is his natural beings and the other one is his serial environment-anthropogenic environment which is created by himself using science, technology religion and politics. Often social environment is painted as a villain warring with nature. In fact there is a direct relationship between urbanisation and environmental problem.

General speaking of environment is equated with nature where in physical component of planet, earth, air, water, etc., support and affect the life in the biosphere. Environment includes all the external conditions and influences affecting life and development of an organism.

Assistant Professor of Economics, Government Arts College, Salem - 7.

On the basis of basic structure, environment may be divided into two basic types.

1. Physical environment.
2. Biological environment.

Physical environment consists of three board categories *viz;*

(i) solid;

(ii) liquid; and

(iii) gas which represent the lithosphere (solid earth) the hydrosphere (water component) and the atmosphere respectively.

The biological component of the environment consists of plants (flora) and animal (fauna) including man as an important factor.

Environment in terms of human beings may be divided to two parts.

1. Natural Environment.
2. Man-made Environment.

Man made environment includes a biotic and biotic environment which man-made environment includes social, cultural, economic, political, historical, aesthetic, psychological religions and educational environment.

What is Global Warming?

Global warming refers to the increase in the average temperature of the earth's near surface, air and oceans in recent decades and its projected continuation. The global average air temperature near earth's surface has increased during the last 100 years. The intergovernmental panel on climate changes (IPCC) concludes, "most of the observed increase in globally averaged temperatures since the mid 20th century is very likely due to the observed increase in anthropogenic green housé concentrations" Via the green house effect natural phenomena such as sales variation combined with volcanoes probably had a small warming effect from pre-industrial times to 1950 and a small cooling effect from 1950 onward. These basic conclusions have been endorsed by a least 30 scientific societies and academies of science.

Problems of Global Warming

Climate change is already affecting millions of people, many are forced to do the things that every one else should be doing to conserve forest, curtail excess use of water and roll back pollution.

Global warming can alter the local environment in important ways for *e.g.*, By changing rainfall patterns or eroding coast lines. Higher temperature can also deplete snow packs and glaciers, which have been reliable sources of water. The Gangotri Glacier in the Himalayas is retreating at a speed of about 30 meters per year. If warming continues these will be excess water flowing in the rivers.

Sea level rise may have a physical impact on coastal areas and island states. India's long coast line of over 6000 km., is densely populated. Several million people may be affected by rise in sea level. By the end of this century there will be a sea level rise of half a meter. The UN World Resource Index 1988 figures out the Indian ocean sector as the most densely populated coastal region in the world, with 135 persons per sq. km. Large population along these coast lines depend on fishing for their livelihood. The temperature on earth is regulated by system known as the Green house effect. Green house gases primary water vapor, carbon dioxide, methane and nitrous oxide trop the heat of sun, preventing radiation from dissipating into space. Over the past 200 years, emission of these gases due to human activities have accumulated in the atmosphere, where because of their long life they stay for anywhere from decades to centuries.

Rising the global temperature may trigger a series of changes with the overall global climate system. Such impacts of climate change could have far reaching and unpredictable environmental social and economic consequences around the world, climate change is projected to:

- Threaten the worlds boreal forest with an increased fire risk because of the drying climate.
- Cause water needs to outstrip supply.

- Cause severe water losses due to changes in evaporation and precipitation patterns.
- Cause flood damage to low-Lying countries and island states. Including loss of coastal land to rising sea level.

Types of Environmental Damages

Water Pollution

> "As a resource, water is an Asset, As a flood it is a threat, As it becomes scarce it causes Drought".

Water is the most precious natural resource for existence of life on the earth. The percapita demand for water in many countries is steadily increasing. A United Nations report has ranked India a poor 120th country for water quality among 122 countries. Chemical pollution of ground water by fluorides spreading epidemic. These fluorides lying dormant in the geological formations, polluting the reservoir water. This is a typical example of an unforeseen health problem created by a project.

Air Pollution

> "Don't breath air in the developed countries Don't drink water in the under developed countries".

The major cause of air pollution in the urban areas are automobiles which inefficiently burn Petroleum releases 75 per cent of air and 80 per cent of nose pollution according to WHO, "The presence of materials in the air in such concentration which are harmful to man and his environment". Urbanisation and Industrialisation is responsible for air pollution. In Delhi it is estimated the at one person dies every hour due to air pollution.

Noise Pollution

With the growth of population and Urbanisation the number of automobiles and other vehicles have increased which produce irritable noise. The noise of communities or social gatherings are no less injurious to our health. Different festivals, processions, crackers, marriages, meetings, rallies etc., produce noise by way of chanting slogans, high pitch music, dancing, speeches, songs and micro phones. Noise mostly affect the work and people in hospitals, schools and libraries etc., where peaceful atmosphere is highly essential.

Soil Pollution

Land has many things to many persons

- to the farmers, livelihood;
- to the town man space to build house;
- to the child a playground;
- to the poet a theme;
- to the patriot a symbol;
- to the economist a valuable resource.

The man-land ratio clearly shows the pressure of population is increasing at alarming rate in cities. The flow of people from villages per day is estimated to 2000, 800 and 400 respectively for Kolkata, Mumbai and Chennai. And also the soil were polluted due to use of fertiliser and pesticides. It create adverse effect to the plants and also human beings.

Impact of Global Warming in Economic Development

Global Warming and Agriculture

Global warming can change the agricultural environment. If Warming continues these will be excess water flowing in the rivers. But once this source being to dry periods resulting in very little water flowing down into life giving rivers.

In our country's economy are largely agriculture and heavily dependent on rainfall could be the worst affected. Changes in temperature and rainfall patterns will directly affect agriculture and food scarcity too. A most two thirds of Indian agriculture is heavily dependent on natural factor such as rainfall. Millions in India would be affected if the cycle or rains get disrupted.

Global Warming and Natural Calamaties

Warmer temperatures could lead to rose in sea level, rise in sea level may have a physical impact on coastal areas and Island states. Global warming may cause the heavy natural calamities like Tsunami, earth quake, heavy rain and heavy flood. The increasing global temperature. The rise in sea surface temperatures could also influence the distribution of marine fish species. The global warming can also deplete snow packs and glaciers which have been reliable sources of water. The Gangotri glacies in the Himalayas for example in retreating at a speed of about 30 meters per year. If warming continues these will be excess water in the rivers.

Global Warming and Marine Production

Global warming could also influence the distribution of marine fish species. If in response to warmer ocean temperature, fish of the coast of India, that would dramatically impact fishing communities in southern state. The UN WRI's (World Resource Index) 1988 figures on the Indian ocean sector as the most densely populated coastal region in the world, with 135 persons per sq. km. Large population along these coast lines depend on fishing for their livelihood and nutrition.

Global Warming and Economic Growth

Developing countries like India that are battling population growth and poverty are the most vulnerable to the impacts of climate change. Ironically most developing economics are also heavily dependent on climate sensitive sectors like agriculture, forestry and fishing. Many of these countries are facing challenges of poverty alleviation and economic growth. The growing impact of climate change will only aggravate their problems. In India where minimum temperature are a small increase in temperature would be felt far more severely here than countries of temperate climate.

Global Warming and Economic Inequality

Global warming is also increasingly become a more political battle between the rich and poor countries, as well as between the rich and poor citizens with in nations. India for example has argued that rich nations which are responsible for most of the population, and whose development was made possible by consuming fossil fuels. But this is a logic that is not applied with in India itself these, poor communities continue to be disadvantaged by consumption of the rich and increased consumption itself is offered as the only hope for millions to rise out of poverty.

Global Warming and Health

Global warming have two opposing direct effects on mortality; Huge temperature on winter reduce death from cold; higher air temperature also increase the concentration of ozone at ground level. Which acts a pollutant in the lower atmosphere. Ozone damages lung tissue and causes particulars problems for people with asthma and oher lung diseases.

Conclusion

At last environment crises and Global warming in the greatest crises of the day. To check the degradation of the environment and to restore the balance in nature is the most important. Challenge to human race. The present and future impacts of global warming have sensitized all the nations. So all the nations should make necessary steps to our earth healthy again.

References

1. The Times of India, Just 8 Years to Fight Global Warming (2007) May 5 Environmental Concerns of India C.P.R. Environment Education Centre.
2. Srivastava Y.N. (1989) Environmental Pollution. Ashish Publishing House, New Delhi.
3. www.environment.in
4. www. Globallwarming.org.
5. University News Vol. 45 No. 44 Oct. 29 - Nov. 04 2007 Special Issues.

16

Global Warming and Agricultural Challenges

Dr. T. Sarathy*
N. Saravanadevi**

Introduction

Global warming is the unusually rapid increase in Earth's average surface temperature over the past century primarily due to the greenhouse gases released as people burn fossil fuels. Since the Industrial Revolution began in about 1750, carbon dioxide levels have increased nearly 38 per cent as of 2009 and methane levels have increased 148 per cent. Temperature histories suggest that global temperature is warmer now than it has been in the past 1,000 years. Temperatures are certain to go up further. The predicted rate of warming for the next century is at least 20 times faster. This rate of change is extremely unusual. Volcanic activity has also, in the deep past, increased greenhouse gases over millions of years, contributing to episodes of global warming. Heat waves, droughts, and intense rain events have increased in frequency during the last 50 years.

* B.E., M.B.A., M. Phil., Ph.D., Assistant Professor, Prims, Periyar University, Salem.

** M.B.A., M.Phil., Assistnant Professor Cum Head, Department of Business Administration, Government Arts College (Autonomous), Salem - 7.

Utilisation of natural resources in a way that nature's equilibrium balance is not affected of its five important forces, the Sky (atmosphere), Sun, Earth, Water and Air. These are also resources which sustain habitat. Over use of one or improper use of another affects balance and creates unusual natural calamities, which is now called as 'Global Warming'. Unabated global warming will reduce global agricultural capacity to a greater extent. Moreover, agriculture accounts for a much larger share of GDP in developing countries than in industrial countries, so a given percentage loss in agricultural potential would impose a larger income loss in a developing country than in an industrial country. For India, prospective losses are massive (as large as about 40%). As India basically agriculture nation nearly 70 per cent of the population is earning for livelihood through agriculture. Large areas are dependent of the rains for farming, the absent and irregular rains hit the farmers hard. As Earth warms up, one of the biggest concerns is the effect on agriculture.

- Vidharba region in the state of Maharashtra in news for the last few years because of the continuous suicides by farmers due to drought.
- Loss of paddy crops in Andhra Pradesh and Tamil Nadu due to frequent flood.
- Thousands of farmers suicide due to loss of crops and inability to repay agri loans.

As Earth warms up, one of the biggest concerns is the effect on agriculture. Thus an attempt is made to bring answers to:

- How will higher temperatures, extreme weather such as droughts, storms, and floods affect agricultural production?
- What are the ways to protect crores of poors who depend on small-scale and subsistence farming?

The world today faces two major challenges to deal effectively with the situation. The first is to reduce carbon dioxide emissions drastically by moving to renewable technologies. The second is to equip ourselves to deal with the impacts of climate change that are already inevitable due to existing levels of greenhouse gases in the atmosphere and excess emission of carbon dioxide.

Agricultural Challenges

Global warming can affect agriculture in a variety of ways. Beyond a certain range of temperatures, warming tends to reduce yields because crops speed through their development, producing less grain in the process. And higher temperatures also interfere with the ability of plants to get and use moisture. Evaporation from the soil accelerates when temperatures rise and plants increase transpiration – that is, lose more moisture from their leaves. The combined effect is called 'evapotranspiration'. Because global warming is likely to increase rainfall, the net impact of higher temperatures on water availability is a race between higher evapotranspiration and higher precipitation. Typically, that race is won by higher evapotranspiration. Heavy rain fall in some areas and the flood cause huge damages to the crops. Due to deforestation very low rainfall and unusual monsoon lead to increased dry lands. Ultimately agricultural production stands unpredicted.

Loss May Amount to one Third of Total Agri-Production

India may meet with losses ranging from about 30 to 40 per cent. It is high time to emphasis importance of co-ordinated international action to limit carbon dioxide emissions and avert warming and damage that will likely otherwise occur, not only in agriculture but also from sea level rise. In India, the arrival and performance of the monsoon plays a significant role in agriculture, as most of the states in the country largely depend upon rainfall for irrigation. Any change in rainfall patterns poses a serious threat to agriculture, and therefore to the country's economy and food security. It is predicted by scientists that global warming could make this already fickle weather system volatile. Agriculture will be adversely affected not only by an increase or decrease in the overall amounts of rainfall, but also by shifts in the rainfall. Pre-monsoon showers in May and June are vital to ensure adequate moisture in fields for rice crops. Worse still are the coastal regions of Gujarat and Maharashtra where inundation and Salinization pose a major hazard. Changes in the soil condition, pests and weeds brought by climate change will also inversely affect agriculture in India. For instance, the amount of moisture in the soil will be affected by changes in factors such as precipitation, runoff and evaporation.

High yield states like Punjab, Haryana and Uttar Pradesh will suffer a decrease of 10 per cent in wheat yield, if winter temperature increases by 0.5°C. The data of onset of summer monsoon over Central India may become more variable. Due to increase in temperature the South Western parts of India receive more rainfall. As a result floods destroy nearly 40 per cent of paddy crops in Andhra Pradesh and Tamil Nadu.

India is expected to lose 125 million tones (about 18%) of its rain fed cereal production potential. If agriculture production goes down, the price of staple food commodities will increase. According to World Bank study, a 2°C rise in temperature along with a 7 per cent increase in rainfall will reduce net agriculture revenues by 12.3 per cent for the whole country. Agriculture in the coastal regions of Gujarat Maharashtra and Karnataka will be severely affected. An increase in minimum temperature from 18°C to 19°C will result in a decrease in rice yield of 0.71 tonne per hectare, while an increase from 22°C to 23°C will result in a decrease of 0.41 tonne per hectare. According to scientists, some positive effects of climate change may also be expected because of increase in CO_2 in the atmosphere, which may have fertilizing effect on crop growth and yields.

> "Ketupathuum Kettarkkuch Chaivaymat Ranke
> Edupathuum Ellam Malai."
>
> **— Thirukkural**

'Want of rain spells ruin; suffiency of it, in turn, will lead to renewed prosperity'.

In fact it is not merely failure of rain, drought, that destroys the crops and ruins people. Even excess rain or cyclone and floods sometimes brings about disaster. We have seen it happen in Andhra Pradesh, Assam, Bihar and Uttar

Pradesh agriculture. Timely rain in moderation and even in reasonable plenty, will alone ensure prosperity and developments in agriculture.

Climate Change and Agricultural Sustainability

Climate change can impact agricultural sustainability in two interrelated ways: *first,* by diminishing the long-term ability of agro-eco-systems to provide food and fiber for the world's population; and *second,* by inducing shifts in agricultural regions that may encroach upon natural habitats. Global warming may encourage the expansion of agricultural activities into regions now occupied by natural ecosystems such as forests. Forced encroachments of this sort may thwart the processes of natural selection of climatically-adapted native crops and other species. If corbon emissions are not curbed the agriculture productivity will affect dramatically especially in developing countries. 2010 was the warmest year ever in India since weather records began in 1901. The Indian Meteorological Department announced that the mean annual temperature in the country during 2010 was as much as 0.93 degrees Celsius higher than the long-term (1961-90) average.

Tea Flavour Fallout Due to Climate Change

Tea growers want the Indian government to fund studies to examine the flavor fallout from climate change. Assam produces nearly 55 per cent of the tea crop in India, a nation that accounts for 31 per cent of global tea production. But the region's tea production has dipped significantly, and plantation owners fear it will drop further as temperatures rise and rainfall patterns change. Assam produced 564,000 tonns of tea in 2007, but slipped to 487,000 tonns in 2009. The 2010 crop is estimated to be about 460,000 tonns, said Dhiraj Kakaty, who heads the Assam Branch Indian Tea Association, an umbrella group of some 400 tea plantations.

Rising Sea Levels Due to Global Warming Its Impact on Agriculture

The major challenges for India in terms of global warming lie in rising sea levels, melting glaciers and agricultural impacts.

Global warming is causing the Gangotri glacier to recede at an annual rate of 30 metres, and the Pindari glacier is retreating at a rate of 13 metres per year. In recent years, extreme weather events like floods, droughts and catastrophe like the Mumbai floods have increased and are probable to rise drastically in the coming decades. Central and Northern India is projected to get less rainfall because of global warming and climate change. In West Bengal, Sunderban mangrove swamps may be affected because of sea level rise. Rising sea levels, salt marshes and mudflats in the Rann of Kutch, the habitat of the greater Flamingoes in Asia may be submerged. About 2000 Indian wild asses could lose their only habitat in India.

About one metre rise in sea level may displace approximately 7.1 million people in India. Because of sea level rise, the entire population of Lakshadweep is at risk. Wet areas could become wetter and dry areas could become drier. Degradation of soil and water resources is one of the main challenges for global agriculture. Climate change will further alter agriculture systems with dangerous consequences for food production and the risk of reduced food yields is greatest in developing countries, where at present 790 million people are estimated to be undernourished.

Eco-systems that cannot move northwards at a rate dictated by global warming will be most at risk. These include, glacial eco-systems, coral reefs, atolls, forests and Himalayan systems. Indian winters may experience a decline of 5-25 per cent in rainfall. More intense rainfall spells are expected in a warmer atmosphere. If rainfall decreases, water flow of rain fed rivers will decrease affecting ground water recharge. Increase in rainfall might aggravate flood situations, bringing destruction of crops and disease.

India is Unprepared

The plight of Indian farmers are flashed across every news channel as India's monsoon rains have failed to arrive and farmers in the worst hit regions resort to suicide to stave off the huge loans they have taken out. Food prices are set to escalate and the dilemma of the country's poorest farmers are becoming a big concern. India is as unprepared to meet the challenge of global warming, which is on its way, as it was the hour before the tsunami struck. Unless the wheels of the state turn quickly, the failure of nature could well turn into a man-made tragedy.

False Panacea

There are some people who argue that rapid technological change will raise agricultural yields so much by late this century that any reduction caused by global warming would easily be more than offset. But technological change is a false panacea for several reasons. The green revolution has already slowed elsewhere. Warmer global temperatures are already causing profound changes in many of the earth's natural systems. Approximately 20-30 per cent of plant and animal species assessed so far are likely to be at increased risk of extinction if increases in global average temperature exceed 1.5-2.5°C.

Need of the Hour

> "Chulanrumerp Pinnadhu Ulagam Adhanal
> Ulandrum Ulave Thalai".
>
> **— Thirukkural**

'The world depends on the poough, more than on any other vocation in life; Despite hardships, therefore agriculture is still the best'.

Ultimately the world depends very much only on agriculture, because that is the most vitally necessary and really productive vocation of all.

The 2009 United Nations Climate Change Conference, commonly known as the Copenhagen Summit, was held at the Bella Centre in Copenhagen, Denmark, between 7 December and 18 December. The Copenhagen declared that climate change is of the greatest challenges of the present day and that actions should be taken to keep any temperature increases to below 2°C.

Conclusion

Public will have to actively support political action, particularly on issues of global climate change, agriculture has long provided adequate quantities of low-cost, healthy food for domestic consumption and substantial quantities for export. Agriculture's ability to continue meeting those needs is challenged by global warming and emerging domestic constraints on land use, water availability, and the environment. Each soul should contribute to the maximum for the mitigation of global warming and improved agricultural production so as to feed the unlimited ever growing population.

References

1. 'Global Warming and Climate Change' (2004), by Agarval S.K., A P H Publishing House.
2. 'Global Warming; Causes, Effects and the Future' (2007), Publisher – Voyager Press.
3. 'Issues in National and International Agriculture' (2008), by Dr. Prabakaran ICFAI University Press.
4. "Forget the Chill, 2010 was India's Hottest year on Record" The Times of India – January 14, 2011.
5. "Thirukkural with English Translation and Explanation" – 2000, Dr. S.M. Diaz and Dr. N. Mahalingam.

17

Does Carbon Emission Leads to Economic Growth Rate in India

Dr. V. S Renukanthan

The linkage between trade and environment can be assessed through the impact of economic growth on environment. Environmental Kuznets Curve (EKC) is commonly applied to examine the impact of economic growth on environment was popularised by Grossman and Krueger (1993). The EKC is a hypothesised relationship between various indicators of environmental degradation and per-capita income. The curve indicates an inverted U shaped function of per-capita income and environmental degradation. The EKC hypothesis that at low level of income, an increase in gross domestic product (GDP) will lead to increase in pollution and as GDP grows pollution shall come at a sustainable limit.

The opening of the economy in India since 1991 has lead to the acceleration of economic growth and since then the economy is growing at an average of eight per cent per year. Hence it is important to assess the economic growth in relation to environmental degradation. The present study aims to investigate the influence of economic growth on environmental degradation and its quality in India.

Associate Professor of Economics, Government Arts College, Salem 636 007, Tamil Nadu.

The present study is organized in five sections. Section *one* provides introduction to EKC and economic growth. Section *two* reviews the related literature on the relationship between economic activities and environment. Section *three* is devoted to empirical model. Section *four* brings out the results and findings and Section *five* provides conclusion of the study.

Review of the Literature

Stern. D.S (2004) presents critical history of environmental Kuznets curve. He finds that recent evidence shows that developing countries addressing environmental issues, sometimes adopting developed countries standard with a short time lag or sometimes better than some wealthy countries and that EKC results have a very flimsy statistical foundation. Managi. S (2004) examines the empirical hypothesis whether free trade is harmful or beneficial for the environment. The study finds that trade liberalisation will increase in CO_2 emission with the elasticity of 0.579.

Dinda. S (2005) studies the linkage between environment and economic growth and OECD and non-OECD countries. The study finds that in OECD country group CO_2 emission is the cause of economic growth of the income, where as growth of income is the cause of CO_2 emission in non-OECD country group. In the other words environmental degradation/ pollution level increase as income level rises in non-OECD group.

Mukhopadhyay. K and Chakraborty. D (2005) examines the relation between environment and trade in India with reference to two hypothesis namely pollution heaven hypothesis and factor endowment hypothesis. They conclude that India do not suffer from pollution heaven hypothesis but support factor endowment hypothesis.

Mete. F (2006) inspects the impact of trade openness on pollution and resource depletion in Nigeria. The findings indicates that pollution is positively related to trade intensity and real GSP per sq. Km., while capital to labour ratio and GNP are negatively related to pollution. The total effect of liberalisation are detrimental to the environment.

Fung. K.C and Maechler. A.M (2007) study the relationship between trade liberalisation and the environment. Their study find that the environmental impact of trade liberalisation depends mostly on two factors, namely as the nature of the pollution that is whether it is local, trans boundary or global and on which country liberalises the trade that is whether it is the clean country or dirty country.

Acharyyya. J (2009) investigate the linkage between FDI, economic growth and environment (CO_2) in India .The study indicates significant long-run positive, but marginal impact FDI inflow on GDP growth in India. On the other hand the long-run growth impact of FDI inflow on CO_2 emission is quite large.

Bello. A.K and Abimbola. O.M (2010) examine the influence of economic growth on environmental quality in Nigeria by testing EKC hypothesis. Their study find the non existence of the inverted 'U' EKC in Nigeria by judging the signs and significance of the coefficient of per capita growth and its square.

Managi. S. and Jena. P.R (2010) investigate the environmental productivity and EKC in India. Their results indicate that over all environmental decreases over the time in India and the combined effect of income on environmental productivity is negative.

Data and Methodology

Data for the analysis were collected from world development indicator (World Bank website) and Indian Economic Survey (2010) published by the Government of India. The model employed for the analysis is based on the study of Antweiler. *et al* (2001). They identified four mechanisms namely Trade Intensity, Scale, Composition and Technique Effect by which trade investment liberalisation affect the environment.

Trade intensity or openness is considered to be equal to imports plus exports in the $year_t$ divide by the GDP in the $year_t$. Thus $(IMP_t+EXP_t)/GDP_t$ = Trade intensity. The composition effect occur when trade leads to specialisation in the sectors where they enjoy comparative advantage or in other words it is also known as factor endowment hypothesis. Composition effect is measured by K_t/L_t where K_t is the capital at time 't' and L_t is the labour or total labour force at time 't'.

Scale effect occurs when liberalisation causes the expansion of economic activity. Scale effect is measured in terms of real GDP per sq. km. That is real GDP/KM^2. The technique effect is measured by real gross national product (real GNP).

Generally time series have been applied in economic for empirical investigation. However one should ensure that for valid inference, all series are integrated in the same order to avoid the problem of spurious relationship and erroneous conclusion (Grranger. G.W and New Bold. P 1993). Most of the economic theories generally explain long-run phenomena. In line with this definition the co-integration explains long-run relationship between variables. While Error Correction Model (ECM) or Vector Error Correction Model (VECM) captures both short-run and long-run relationship between variables. As Granger (1986) points out if two variables are co-integrated then Granger causality must be at least in one direction. The test of co-integration and causality between two or more variables consists of two steps. The *first* step is to test the unit root condition or to verify the order of integration, since causality tests are valid if variables have some order of integration. Unit root test check non-stationary of variables and of it is found non-stationary the variable has to be integrated of zero I(0) to achieve stationary. This can be accomplished by Augmented Dickey fuller (ADF) test. The ADF test is based on the following regression equation.

$$\Delta X = \alpha_0+\beta_1 X_{t-1}+\sum_{i=1}^{k} \beta_2 \Delta X_{t-1}+\varepsilon_t \qquad \text{———— Equation 1}$$

Where Δ refers to first difference operator, X the variable to be differenced, that is:

$\Delta X = X-X_{t-1}$ α, β and β_2 are co-efficient and ε the error term. The null hypothesis of existence of unit root is $\beta_1 = 0$. To allow the possible presence of deterministic time trend the equation (1) is augmented with time trend component in order to test the presence of unit root, then equation (1) becomes where 'T is linear trend and 'k' in the equation (1) and (2) indicates optimal lag based on Akaike Info Criterion (AIC).

$$\Delta X = \alpha_0 + \lambda T + \beta_1 X_{t-1} + \Sigma_{i=1}^{k} \beta_2 \Delta X_{t-1} + \varepsilon_t \quad \text{——— Equation 2}$$

The *second* step is to test existence of co-integration of variable to know the long-run relationship between variables and generally in research Johanson test (1978) procedure is employed. If the long-run relationship exists between the variables then they are said to be co-integrated. The present study uses Johanson multivariate produce testing co-integration. The Johanson maximum likelihood allows testing multivariate frame works and avoids some of the drawbacks of Engle Granger (1987) co-integration methodology. Given the variables are co-integrated, their pattern of causality should be tested in the context of an Error Correction Model (ECM) is one of the importance of ECM strategy in that the estimation procedure takes in to account the short and long-run dynamics of the system. Based on the ECM, Johanson and Juselius (1990) Model can be defined as:

$$\Delta Y_t = \alpha + \lambda_{et-1} + \beta_1 \Delta Y_{t-1} + \ldots\ldots + \beta_p \Delta Y_{t-p} + W_0 \Delta X_{t-1} + \ldots\ldots W_q \Delta X_{t-q} + \varepsilon_t \quad \text{——— Equation 3}$$

Where Δ is the difference operator, β and W are parameters to be estimated, λ_{et-1} is error correction term and ε_t is vector random error, ΔY_{t-1} and ΔX_{t-1} are the explanatory variables. The following equation models are fitted based on equation (3) for the present study.

The model for the study is specified as:

$$POL_t(CO_2) = \alpha + \beta(IMP_t + EXP_t)/GDP_t) + \lambda(K_t/L_t) + \phi(RGDP_t/KM^2) + \psi(RGNP_t) + \mu$$

Where POL_t is yearly quantity of carbon-di-oxide emission and all others are as mentioned above. μ is error term.

ADF and PP test results are not given. These results can be obtained from the author by request.

Table 17. 1 to 17.4 explain the Granger causality test. Table 17.1 reveals that CO_2 is the cause for real GNP. In other words $CO_2 \rightarrow$ RGNP where the arrow points to be direction of causality. This implies that CO_2 leads to increase in real GNP.

Table 17.1:

Pair-wise Granger Causality Tests Lags: 2			
Null Hypothesis:	Obs	F_Statistic	Probability
TE does not Granger Cause CO_2	26	0.32340	0.72722
CO_2 does not Granger Cause TE		4.28723	0.02746

In Table 17.2 indicates that CO_2 emission is the cause for openness of the economy. It is unidirectional causality from CO_2 to OT.

Table 17.2:

Pair-wise Granger Causality Tests Lags: 2			
Null Hypothesis	Obs	F_Statistic	Probability
OT does not Grangdr Cause CO_2	26	0.38638	0.68424
CO_2 does not Granger Cause OT		3.37751	0.05348

Table 17.3 shows that independence of variable scale effect and $CO_{2.}$

Table 17.3:

Pair-wise Granger Causality Tests Lags: 2			
Null Hypothesis	Obs	F_Statistic	Probability
OT does not Grangdr Cause CO_2	26	0.38638	0.68424
CO_2 does not Granger Cause OT		3.37751	0.05348

Table 17.4 reveals unidirectional causality from composition effect to $CO_{2.}$

Table 17.4:

Pair-wise Granger Causality Tests Lags: 2			
Null Hypothesis	Obs	F_Statistis	Probabality
OT does not Grangdr Cause CO_2	26	0.38638	0.68424
CO_2 does not Granger Cause OT		3.37751	0.05348

Table 17. 5 and 17.6 show Johnsen co integration rank test and eigen value. The trace test maximum value shows that there is two and one co integration at 5 per cent level of significance. Hence error correction model is followed.

Table 17. 5:

Series: CE CO_2 OT SER TE Lags interval (in first difference): 1 to 1 Cointegration Rank Test (Trace)				
Hypothesized No. of CE (s)	**Eigen Value**	**Trace Statistic**	**0.05 Critical Value**	**Prob.****
None*	0.780656	93.00783	69.81889	0.0003
At most 1*	0.640160	53.56285	47.85613	0.0132
At most 2	0.501086	26.98836	29.79707	0.1019
At most 3	0.501086	8.909987	15.49471	0.3736
At most 4	0.245139	1.598225	3.841466	0.2062

Trace test indicates 2 cointegrating eqn(s) at the 0.05 leval.

* Denotes rejection of the hypothesis at the 0.05 leval.

** MacKinnon-Haug-Michelis (1999) p-values.

The sign of co efficient of estimate of Ecm_{t-1}, the residual error correction term is negatively and statistically insignificant, which do not support convergence towards long-run equilibrium. This indicates that only 0.03 per cent is of any disequilibrium of CO_2 is of anytime is made up during the current period. Other variables like CE is significant negatively. Overall the model suggest that SE and TE is positively related to CO_2 emission. OT and CO_2 is negatively related, which indicate that openness of trade of trade may reduce CO_2 emission.

Table 17.6: Cointegration Rank Test (Maximum Eigenvalue)

Hypothesized No.of CE (s)	Eigen value	Trace Statistic	0.05 Critical Value	Prob.**
None*	0.780656	39.44498	33.87687	0.0098
At most 1	0.640160	26.57448	27.58434	0.0669
At most 2	0.501086	18.07838	21.13162	0.1269
At most 3	0.245139	7.311762	14.26460	0.4529
At most 4	0.059619	1.598225	3.841466	0.2062

Max-eignvalue test indicates 1 cointegrating eqn(s) at the 0.05 level.
* Denotes rejection of the hypothesis at the 0.05 level.
** MacKinnon-Haug-Michelis (1999) p-values.

Conclusion

The study finds that increase in CO_2 emission does lead economic growth. The growth of industries and weak implementation of environment law has raised the level of CO_2 emission paving the way for global warming in significantly. Hence it is necessary to reduce the level of gas emission with the adoption of new technology and clean development mechanism so that India can save itself from becoming heaven for pollution industry.

References

1. Acharyya. J. (2009), "FDI, Growth and the Environment: Evidence from India on Co_2 Emission During lost Two Decades," *Journal of Economic Development*, Vol. 34, pp. 43-58.
2. Antweiler. W. *et al.*, (2001), "Is Free Trade Good for Environment?. *The American Economic Review* 4 (2), 877-908.
3. Bello. A. K. and Apimola. O. M. (2010), "Does Level of Economic Growth Influence Environmental Quality in Nigeria: A Test of Environmental Kuznets Curve (EKC) Hypothesis", *Pakistan Journal of Social Science, 7(4),* 325-329.
4. Dinda. S. (2005), "Does Economic Link to Economic Growth", An International Workshop, Asker, Near Oslo, 21-23 June. 2005.
5. Fung. K. C. and Maechler. A. M. (2007), "Trade Liberalisation and the Environment: The Case of Intra – Industry Trade",

Journal of International Trade and Economic Development, Vol. 16, No. 1, pp. 53-69.

6. Granger. C.W.J. and New Bold. P (1974), "Spurious Regression in Economics", *Journal of Econometrics, 2,* pp. 111-120.
7. Granger. C.W.J. (1986), "Development in the Study of Co-integrated Economics Variables", *Oxford Bulletin of Economics and Statistics*, 48, 213-228.
8. Johansen. S. (1988), "Statistical Analysis of Co-integration Vectors", *Journal of Economic Dynamics and Control"*, 12, 231-254.
9. Johansen. S. (1991), "Estimation and Hypothesis Testing of Co-integration Vector in Gaussian Vector Auto Regression Models", *Econometrica*, 59, 1151-1158.
10. Managi. S. and Jena. P.R. (2005), "Environmental Productivity and Kuzbets Curve in India", *Journal of eco le con.*
11. Managi. S. (2004), "Trade Liberalisation and the Environment: Carbon – di – oxide for 1960-99", *Economic Bulletin* Vol. 17 No. 1 pp. 1-15.
12. Mete. F. (2007), "Impact of Trade Liberalisation as the Environment in Developing Countries: The Case of Nigeria" MPRA Paper No. 371.
13. Mukhopadhyay. K and *et al.*, (2005), "Pollution Heaven and Factor Hypothesis, Revisited: Evidence from India" – Paper Submitted in the 15th International Input-output Conference 2005 at Renmin University in Beijing – China.
14. Quershi. M.S. (2006), Trade Liberalisation, Environment and Poverty, UNU-WIDER, Research Paper No. 2006/45.
15. Stern. D.I. (2004), "The Rise and Fall of Environmental Kuznets Curve", *World Development* Vol. 32, No. 8, pp. 1419-1439.

18

Impact of Global Warming on Agricultural Production

Dr. S. Chandrasekaran

In the long list of potential problems from global warming, the risks to world agriculture stand out as among the most important. Yet there has been a tendency in the climate economics literature in recent years to downplay this risk, and even to argue that a couple of degrees Celsius warming might benefit world agriculture. But such studies typically have too short a time horizon (generally out to about 2050). They also focus on overall temperature change (which includes oceans), rather than on the changes that will occur over land (which warms more easily and quickly than water) – and specifically agricultural land.

It has been widely recognised that developing countries in general stand to lose more from the effects of global warming on agriculture than do industrial countries. Most developing countries have less capacity to adapt than do their wealthier neighbors. Most are in warmer parts of the globe, where temperatures are already close to or beyond thresholds at which further warming will reduce rather than increase

Associate Professor and Head Department of Economics, Government Arts College, Salem - 7.

agricultural output. Agriculture is a larger share of developing economies than of industrial economies. But it has been difficult to estimate just how much individual countries are likely to be affected.

How Climate Affects Agriculture

Climate change can affect agriculture in a variety of ways. Beyond a certain range of temperatures, warming tends to reduce yields because crops speed through their development, producing less grain in the ability of plants to get and use moisture. Evaporation from the soil accelerates when temperatures rise and plants increase transpiration, lose more moisture from their leaves. The combined effect is called 'evapotranspiration'. Because global warming is likely to increase rainfall, the net impact of higher temperatures on water availability is a race between higher evapotranspiration and higher precipitation. Typically, that race is won by higher evapotranspiration.

The Impact on Crop Yields

The results give little support to the optimists. Globally, the overall impact of baseline global warming by the 2080s is a reduction in agricultural productivity (output per hectare) of 16 per cent without carbon fertilization, and a reduction of 3 per cent should carbon fertilization benefits actually materialize-when results are weighted by output. The losses are greater when weighted by population or country.

The sharp concentration of losses is in the developing countries. Whereas the industrial countries experience outcomes ranging from 6 per cent losses without carbon fertilization to 8 per cent gains with it, developing country regions suffer losses of about 25 per cent without carbon fertilization and 10-15 per cent if carbon fertilization is included. For developing countries, the median loss would be 15-26 per cent, and the output-weighted average loss, 9-21 per cent. Losses could reach devastating levels in some of the poorest countries.

In Asia, two largest and most dynamic developing countries is stark. India produces perhaps the most disturbing single set of results, with losses ranging from about 30 to 40 per cent. China would have a more moderate range, from a 7 per cent loss to a 7 per cent gain. Its results resemble those of the United States. In both countries, the average effects are relatively neutral, but there are sizable losses in the southern regions. The contrast with India is strictly consistent with India's location closer to the equator. Both china and the United States have a latitude centre of about 38° north, whereas India's latitude centre is about 22° north.

The developing countries are most at risk, so it is strongly in their own interest that they participate actively in international abatement programmes. China already produces larger carbon dioxide emissions than the European Union and will soon surpass those of he United States. Global emissions from developing countries (including from deforestation) are already equal to those from industrial countries, and are growing faster.

It is striking that the two largest developing countries, India and China, seem to have potentially conflicting interests in their approach to international abatement efforts. With broadly neutral or even positive effects on its agriculture, China could be less interested in international efforts to restrain emissions than India, which faces major potential losses if there is no change in global emissions policies. But even in China, some key subregions are at risk.

Impact on Agriculture

There are almost 500,000 farmers in the country who are shifting to organic farming. The gains from green revolution have been proved unsustainable and unviable. The agricultural productivity has reached a plateau. The high cost of production compounded with small land holding size and competition from cheaper imports are making agriculture an unviable livelihood option. The air, soil and water pollution, caused by chemical inputs has severely affected the lives of the villages, their resources and the delicate food chain. All these reasons have compelled farmers, civil society and agricultural scientists to search for a farming system which ensures sustainability of the whole agricultural ecology and viability of production system. Among all farming systems, organic farming is gaining wide attention. The reasons being it's low cost, high quality and healthy produce, cleaner environment and above all its suitability to traditional knowledge and local agro-climatic conditions.

In organic farming, traditional practices of farming like crop rotations, mixed cropping are exercised in which inputs are in the form of available organic waters and other biological material. Both the practices and inputs keep the soil in good health by increasing its organic content; control pest attack without polluting environment and food chain and also lead to better waster use efficiency. All these factors not only reduce cost of production but also ensure sustainable production. For consumers, 'organic' is a labeling term, which is perceived as safer, healthier, environment – friendly and socially responsible. For traders 'organic' is yet another specially product for niche marks which commands premium price. In the market of developed countries.

Agriculture is one of the most Weather-dependent of all human activities. In India, agriculture and allied activities constitute the single largest component of Gross Domestic Product (GDP) contributing nearly 25 per cent of the total. The tremendous importance of this sector to the Indian economy can be ganged by the fact that it provides employment to two-thirds of the total workforce. The share of agricultural products in exports is also substantial, with agriculture accounting for 15 per cent of export earnings. Agricultural growth also has a direct impact on poverty eradication, and is an important factor in employment generation. Further, Indian agriculture is fundamentally dependent on weather for higher productivity.

India, as a developing country has reasons to be concerned about the adverse impact of climate change on its economy. A large part of its population depends on climate sensitive sectors for livelihoods which makes it highly vulnerable to climate change. Climate change can have serious impact on its crops, forests, coastal regions, etc., which can in turn affect the achievement of its important national development goals. The issue of climate change cannot however be taken up without linking it to developmental needs such as poverty, health, energy access and education. Efforts to address climate change adaptation and mitigation needs should not take resources away from the core development needs and growth objectives of the developing countries. Climate Change mitigation and poverty reduction should be addressed simultaneously.

Impact of Climate Change in Agriculture

Agriculture is the mainstay of Indian economy and provides food and livelihood security to a substanitial section of the Indian population. The impact of climate change as witnessed in recent times has immense potential to adversely affect agriculture in this country in a variety of ways. As a large part of the arable land in India is rain-fed, the productivity of agriculture depends on the rainfall and its patterns. Agriculture will be adversely affected not only by an increase or decrease in the rainfall patterns but poses a serious threat and the food security of the economy. Summer rainfall accounts for almost 70 per cent of the total annual rainfall over India and is crucial to Indian agriculture.

Rise in temperature caused by increasing green house is likely to affect crops differently from region to region. As a result of climate change the amount of arable land in high-latitude region is likely to increase by reduction of the amount of frozen lands. At the same time arable land along the coast lines are bound to be reduced as a result of rising sea level. Erosion, submergence of shorelines, salinity of the water table due to the increased sea levels, could mainly affect agriculture through inundation of low lying lands.

Agriculture will be adversely affected not only by an increase or decrease in the overall amounts of rainfall, but also by shifts in the timing of the rainfall. Higher temperatures reduce the total duration of a crop cycle, leading to a lower yield per unit area, especially for India's wheat and paddy crops. Soil erosion, increased numbers of pests and weeds brought by climate change will also affect agriculture in India. For instance, the amount of moisture in the soil will be affected by changes in factors such as rainfall, runoff and evaporation. Global warming will seriously affect agriculture. Some species of agricultural crops will be adversely affected by higher temperatures, increased weeds and harmful insects. It is also possible that global warming will lead to global food shortages.

The Food and Agricultural Organization (FAO) has warned that India could lose up to 125 million tones of cereals. The Intergovernmental panel on Climate Change (IPCC) which was awarded Nobel prize in he year 2008 has warned that due to global warming, the sea levels in Asia will rise by at least 40cm by 2100 flooding vast areas on the coastline, including some of the most densely populated cities, whose population will be forced to migrate inland (The Hindu Business Line dated 03-11-2007). The first to be affected by the climate change will be those living in the fringe zones, working outdoors or whose livelihoods depend directly on the physical environment. Viewed from these perspectives, the main sectors facing from direct impact could be agriculture, water resources and health.

The IPCC report indicates high probability of crop losses with increases in temperature in the tropical regions. Studies do confirm this trend. Among cereal crops important for food security, wheat is most sensitive to even small increase in temperature. Relatively, rice has greater tolerance to temperature increases. Increasing climate variability could result in considerable season/annual fluctuation in food production. All agricultural commodities are subject to such variability.

19

Global Warming

Impact and Care

Dr. P. Ambiga Devi*
Dr. K. Shobha**
K. R. Gomathi***

Global warming is a major environmental problem. It is the process by which the mean global temperature is increased due to increased concentration of chlorofluorocarbons (CFCs) formed mainly from industrial smoke and vehicular emissions. India in the developing process, needs more energy to bring structural changes in the production process. To generate electricity, India has to burn fossil fuels, as 70 per cent of our electricity supply comes from coal. Burning of fossil fuels alone account for 83 per cent of India's carbon-di-oxide emissions which add to GHG's leading to global warming. Since the beginning of the industrial revolution human activities have caused an increase in several GHG's most notably carbon-di-oxide. Another cause is land use changes, such as deforestation. When forest land is destroyed. Carbon-di-oxide is released into the air. It is reported that 25 per cent of all

* Professor of Economics, Avinashilingam Deemed University for Women.

** Associate Professor in Economics, Government Arts College.

*** Research Scholar, Avinashilingam Deemed University for Women, Coimbatore.

carbon-di-oxide release entering the atmosphere is because of cutting and burning of about 34 million acres in a year. If we continue emitting carbon-di-oxide into the atmosphere, it is estimated that by the year 2030, concentration of carbon-di-oxide, will have been doubled from pre industrial revolution.

Impacts of Global Warming

Global warming leads to:

- Rise in temperature.
- Rise in sea level.
- Occurrence of extreme events.

Rise in Temperature

Since warming depends upon the level of GHG's in the atmosphere, continued emission beyond the absorptive capacity of the earth would cause increase in temperature. The National Oceanic and Atmospheric Administration, the climate agency of America reported that the average temperature of Earth for the first four months of the year 2010 of 13.3°C is 0.69°C above the 20th century average. The IPCC projected a warming of about 0.2.°C per decade, if emission of GHGs continues to increase at the present rate. In most cases rise temperature is expected to be 2 to 4 °C. Any increase in atmospheric temperature may increase the water requirement of the crops, reduce the crop duration and reduce the yield. The decline in agricultural productivity in India over the years for selected food grains is shown in Table 19.1.

Table 19.1: Trends in Yields of Foodgrains (kg/ha)

Items	1950-51	2001-02	2007-08
Foodgrains	522	1734	1854
Pulses	441	607	638
Rice	688	2079	2203
Wheat	633	2762	2785
Oilseeds	481	913	1086

Source: Economic Survey, Various Issues.

About 80 per cent of Indian farmers supplement agriculture with livestock for enhancing the income and food for sustainability. The rise in temperature would likely result in decline in dairy production, reduced animal weight gain and reproduction and lower feed conversion efficiency in warm regions.

Rise in Sea Level

The rise in temperature leads to a rise in sea level. The sea level along much of the US coast is already rising at the rate of 2.5 to 3.0 mm per year or about 10-12 inches per century. The IPCC (2007) estimated that the rise in global average sea level during 1961-2003 was about 1.8 mm per year; where as during 1993-2003 it was about 3.1 mm per year. The expected rise in sea level by the end of this century is 0.18-0.38 mm and 0.26-0.59 for the low emission and high emission scenario. The causes of rise are thought to be two fold: the primary cause being the thermal expansion of warm ocean water and the secondary cause being the melting of glacial ice. Mountain glaciers and snow cover have declined on an average in both hemi spheres. The rise in the sea level results in the melting of glaciers. Himalayan glaciers are retreating at the rate of 50 feet or 15 meters per year. This increases flood risk and changes in ocean circulation patterns such as the conveyer belt. This could affect and harm plants and animals that live in the sea. These glaciers feed the major rivers of India such as Indus, Ganga and Brahmaputra. The economic impact of loosing these fresh water resources in India could have severe economic impacts on the people as well as on agriculture. This affects fish population and the aquatic food web as species seek conditions suitable for their life. Higher ocean acidity affects the marine environment through deficiency in calcium carbonate, affecting shelled organisms and coral reefs. Exacerbate flooding and increase in the salinity of rivers bays and ground water arise with rise in the sea level.

Occurrence of Extreme Events

The emerging global warming results in uncertain but significant risks of catastrophic outcomes. Severe heat waves, hurricanes, droughts and other erratic weather extremes are part of global warming. A World Bank report estimates that environmental degradation costs India around 80 billion dollars a year in terms of public health. R.K. Pachauri, the Chairman of IPCC (2008) reported that:

- Endemic morbidity and mortality due to diarrhea disease is primarily associated with floods and droughts.
- Exacerbation of the abundance and toxicity of cholera is due to increase in coastal water temperature.
- Increased deaths, disease and injury due to hear waves, floods, storms, fires and droughts.

Measures Undertaken to Mitigate Global Warming

- The Ministry of Renewable Energy is promoting sources of renewable energy.
    - ➢ solar energy;
    - ➢ bio-mass;
    - ➢ hydel energy.
- Wind energy and geothermal energy sources are also being explored.
- Cleaner fuel is also being promoted through administrative and legal ways.
- Educational institutions have included 'environmental science' in their curriculum.
- Public awareness has also been created.
- Water conservation and harvest technologies have been promoted.

Suggestions

Humans directly or indirectly cause global warming. Let us not wait for the governments to find a solution for this problem. There are simple things which an individual can do to reduce the global warming phenomena. Follow the 'three R mantra' – Refuse, Reduce and Reuse.

- *Refuse*
- Boycott firecrackers.
- Use paper bags in shopping malls instead of plastics.

- Use water frugally.
- Buy organic food, educate the rural and urban consumers to go for green products.
- *Reuse*
- Use washable plates and utensils.
- Create alternative energy resources by using the existing technology.
- *Reduce*
- Drive vehicles with good mileage.
- If possible walk or take public transport.
- Replace a regular incandescent light bulb with a compact fluorescent light bulb. CFLs use 60 per cent less energy than a regular bulb.
- Do not leave electrical appliances on stand by mode when not in use. Use the 'on/off' function on the machine itself.
- Turn out the light when leaving the room.
- Have trees around the houses.

Universities have to take up research on climate change, carbon trading and green environment. To conclude.

For the Government

- The central and state governments have to go beyond GDP, to measure and manage the cost of climate change, environmental degradation and bio-diversity loss.

For the Corporate

- The corporates have to sign up the 'Carbon Disclosure Project' in India.

For the Individuals

- Before buying anything ask 'How Eco Friendly It Is'?

References

1. Arun D Sawant (2010), "Climate Change: Impact and Need for Carbon Trading", University News, 48 (24) June 14-20, 2010.
2. UN Intergovernmental Panel on Climate Change (IPCC), Assessment Reports.
3. http://www.climatehotmap.org/asia

20

Global Efforts to Control Climate Change

Dr. C. Dhandapani

Introduction

Climate change refers to the variations in the global or regional climates over time. It often refers to changes in modern climate. According to Inter-governmental Panel on Climate Change (IPCC) which was awarded the Nobel Prize climate changes are 90 to 95 per cent likely to have been caused by human action.

Green House Gas is the primary cause of global warming. Green house gases are also important in understanding earth's climate history. The inter-governmental panel scientists found that the burning of fossil fuels some agricultural practices and changes in land use have been generating green house gases like carbon dioxide, methane and nitrous oxide that trapped heat and produced runaway global warming. If the production of these green house gases continued to soar global temperatures would rise up to 6.4 degree Celsius by the end of this century with far reaching consequences for the climate, warned the IPCC. This paper analyses the causes for climate change, impacts on Indian economy and suggests remedial measures to control climate change.

Associate Professor of Economics, Thiruvalluar University, Vellore - 632 106.

The *first* theory, which is the generally accepted one, is that the release of greenhouse gases from the burning of fossil fuel and from land use is responsible for the recent temperature increase.

The *second* theory is that the sun's magnetic field and the solar wind modulate the amount of high energy cosmic radiation that the earth receives. This in turn affects low altitude cloud cover and how much water vapor there is in the atmosphere and thus regulates the climate.

Green House Effect

Global temperature rise is due to phenomenon of green house effect that was first reported in 1896, by Swedish chemist Arrhenius. The air pollutants responsible for the green house effect are known as the green house gases.

Sources of Green House Gases

Carbon dioxide is the main anthropogenic green house gas. The global atmospheric concentration of carbon dioxide has increased from a pre industrial value of about 280 ppm (parts per million) to 379 ppm in 2005. The atmospheric concentration of carbon dioxide in 2005 exceeded by far the natural range over many thousands of years. The annual carbon dioxide concentration growth rate was larger during the last 10 years. The primary source of the increased atmospheric concentration of carbon dioxide since the pre-industrial period results from fossil fuel use.

Emission of GHG in India

India has the world's second largest population and is the third largest emitter of CO_2 after USA and China according to United Nations Environment Programme. It estimated that India emitted 908 million tones of CO_2 in 1998, four per cent of the world's total. The per capita emissions of CO_2 are 0.93 million tonnes per annum. In 2004, the per capita emission of CO_2 are 1.02 million tonnes per annum were well below the world average of 4.2 per cent million tonnes per annum. Since GHG emissions were directly linked to economic growth, India's economic activities would necessarily involve increased emissions.

Causes for Climate Change

It is well established fact that Climate change is largely due to man made causes and only partly due to natural causes. The human causes are the releases of what are called Green House Gases (GHGs), notably Carbon dioxide emitted by power stations burning coal and automobiles run on petroleum and diesel and nitrogen oxides from vehicular exhausts. There other factors responsible for GHG are paddy cultivation and cattle. Deforestation and forest degradation is a major contributor to climate change, accounting for nearly 20 per cent of total green house gas emissions.

Impact of Climate Change

The concept of climate change is a serious problem. It is feared that the climate change would have a disastrous impact on global climate, human and animal life. The adverse impacts may range from unusually warm summers, warm winters, erratic rainfall, increasing incidences of floods and hurricanes, rising sea levels threatening coastal areas, droughts, water scarcity and poor crop yields.

Global warming would not only lead to loss of life and property, but also might cause a major reshuffle in flora, fauna and cropping pattern in India. Worldwide it is agreed that one of the greatest challenges to sustainable development in the 21st century is climate change. Climate change poses a serious threat to development and poverty reduction in the poorest and most vulnerable regions of the world. Its impact is already being experienced across the globe.

The poor are the most vulnerable to the effects of climate change, having the least recourse from the status quo and minimal physical protection from environmental shifts. Most of India's poor live in rural areas that are directly dependent on climate sensitive resources such as agriculture, forests, and river water. India's diversity of topography-mountains, rivers, forests, deserts, coastlines – means that climate change would affect different regions in different ways.

1. *Rise in Sea Level*

The first and foremost challenge of climate change would be the rise in the mean sea level. According to the IPCC's fourth assessment report that was released on 2nd February 2007, there has been acceleration in sea level since 1993. Between 1961 and 2003, the sea level had increased at an average rate of 0.18 meters per year. But between 1993 and 2003, the rate of rise had nearly doubled to 0.31 meters per year. The report predicted that sea level would increase up to 0.38 meters by the mid of this century and 0.59 meters by the end of the 21st century.

India has a vast coastal line and the rising sea levels caused by climate change would cause an ecological disaster. In India, 207 million families depend on coastal resources. The big cities of Mumbai and Kolkata with large and growing populations and huge investments in infrastructure are located on the coast. Low level areas such as those in Orissa, West Bengal and Lakshadweep islands would be vulnerable to inundation. An increase in sea level would also lead to salt water entering the ground water aquifers on which people depend for drinking water and to irrigate their fields. Valuable marine and coastal ecosystem including mangrove forests, coral reefs, and sea grasses would also get adversely affected by sea level rise. In the sea it would create dead zones with no fish.

2. *Melting of Glaciers*

Majority of mountain glaciers have been shrinking over the pat 150 years. Many glaciers at lower latitudes are now disappearing and scientists predict that under some plausible warming scenarios, majority of glaciers would be gone by the year 2100. It is estimated that glaciers in the Himalayas are shrinking at a rate of 10 to 15 meters per year as a result of the earth warming.

3. *Effect on Nature*

Climate change would also lead to powerful cyclones, hurricanes, droughts, floods, heat waves, storms, heavy rainfall and many other natural disasters which would occur more frequently in many parts of India.

4. *Effect on Temperature*

Since the end of the 19th century, the earth's average surface temperature has increased by 0.3-0.6 degree Celsius. Over the past 40 years, the rise has been 0.2-0.3 degree Celsius. According to Inter-governmental Panel on Climate Change (IPCC), the average global temperature would increase between 1.5 degree Celsius to 4.5 degree Celsius by 2050. Change in temperature and rainfall would bring out a change in the type of vegetation in about 80 per cent of the existing forests in the country. Such changes were bound to have a significant impact on the forest and the wildlife they supported.

A recent report by the scientists has revealed that India has almost consistently experienced more than normal annual mean temperatures for the past 16 years. The Meteorological Department, Pune revealed that India was warming at the rate of 0.48 degrees Celsius over 100 years. The year 2006 was the warmest year on record since 1901.

5. *Climate Change and Agriculture*

India basically an agrarian economy depends on agriculture and allied activities for the economic well being of its more than one billion population of whom nearly 65 per cent lives in rural areas. Climate change will affect agricultural yield directly because of alterations in temperature and rainfall and indirectly through changes in soil quality, pests and diseases particularly, the yield of cereals.

Studies of Indian Agriculture Research Institute indicate that Indian agriculture would face many challenges over the coming years by climate change. Extreme weather conditions such as high temperature, heavy rainfall, floods, droughts, shifting monsoons, drier soils, etc., would reduce the yields of food grains. Recent media reports say that India is likely to be deprived of south-west monsoon in 150 years. Climate change is expected to lead to an intensification of the global hydrological cycle and can have major impacts on regional water resources, affecting both ground and surface water supply.

Thus, degrading soils and water resources could place enormous strains on achieving food security for growing population. World food prices are increasing in the current decade, particularly during 2007-08 reflecting higher demand and low supply. Prices of all food items like rice, wheat, maize, and edible oils increased more than double between 2005 to 2008.

The impact of climate change on food production and crop yields would not only affect physical availability of food but also the incomes of people. Changes in growth and distribution of incomes may affect demand for agricultural produce, which in turn would again affect food production.

Increase in carbon dioxide concentration to 550 parts per million (ppm) could increase yields of rice, wheat, and oilseeds by 10-20 per cent. However, a degree increase in temperature may reduce yield of wheat, soyabean, mustard, groundnut and potato by 3-7 per cent. Sanghi and Mendelsohn have estimated that under moderate climate change scenarios, there would be about 9 per cent decline in farm level net revenues in India.

6. *Effect on Health*

Climate change is a threat to both mankind and any life form existing on planet earth. Climate change would affect human health in many ways. It will have wide-ranging harmful effects including increase in heat-related mortality, dehydration, spread of infectious diseases, malnutrition, and damage to public health.

Warmer temperature would increase the risk of mortality from heat stress. Change in climate causes change in temperature. A sudden change of up to 30-35 degrees coming from high latitudes to the warmth of the tropics may affect the human health. Some times even though the temperature may be bearable, the type and intensity of radiation at certain times of the day may be harmful because of the fragility of the skin, the eye and other parts of the body, Intense UV-radiation, most particularly is to be avoided otherwise it may lead to skin cancer and eye cataract. Exposure to such temperatures may lead to dehydration and even fatality.

It is anticipated that there will be an increase in the number of deaths due to greater frequency and severity of heat waves and other extreme rise in the temperature would affect people living in the urban areas. This is due to the 'heat islands' that develop here owing to the presence of concrete constructions, paved and tarred roads.

Climate change would likely to increase considerably toll of infectious diseases worldwide. High temperature could influence the incidence of diseases such as malaria, dengue fever, yellow fever and several types of encephalitis. Malaria prevalence may increase by 50 million to 80 million cases per year with an associated 3 degree Celsius rise in average global temperature and rainfall patterns and the increase in CO_2 levels projected to accompany climate change would undoubtedly have important effects on global agriculture and thus on human nutrition.

Tropical cyclones can be traumatizing. The fury of hurricane winds and other associated weather can greatly affect the health of the people.

It would also influence the incidence of diseases like malaria, dengue, yellow fever and cholera. According to WHO, there is a potential for increase in air pollution related morbidity and mortality in world population due to the release of GHG. This could result in 50 to 80 million additional deaths per year worldwide by 2100.

The Task Group of WHO has warned that climate change will have serious impacts on human health. Strategies aimed at reducing potential health impacts of anticipated climate changes should include the monitoring of infectious diseases and disease vectors to detect early changes in the incidence of diseases. Environmental management measures may be adopted to reduce risk and to improve disaster preparedness for floods, droughts and their health related problems.

Food consumption and nutrition are affected by climate change through its effects on health and spread of diseases. Poor people are especially vulnerable to the risks of climate change which results in food insecurity and childhood malnutrition. Hence, Government and policy-makers should give priority to social protection measures that focus on early childhood nutrition to mitigate risk associated with reduced food access, particularly for the poorest households.

7. *Effect on Fauna*

Climate change also affects aquatic fauna. Fresh water fishes would migrate pole ward. The habitat for cold water fishes would be destroyed. Many species of fishes would become extinct.

8. *Effect on Migration of People*

Number of people will be displaced, either temporarily or permanently from their homes as a consequence of global warming. It is estimated that a billion people could be permanently displaced by climate change related phenomenon such as droughts, floods and hurricanes. It has been estimated that 70,000 people out of the 4.1 million living in the Indian parts of the suburban islands would be rendered homeless by 2020. They are called environmental refugees. Moreover, climate change might lead to increased flow of migrants from neighboring countries also.

Global Efforts to Control Climate Change

Rio de Janeiro Conference

The UN Framework Convention on Climate Change (UNFCCC) was adopted in 1992 at Rio de Janeiro. The Convention called upon the developed countries to reduce their emissions of GHGs to below their 1990 levels.

The Kyoto Protocol

The Kyoto Protocol of December, 1997, laid down quantitative targets for each of the developed countries to be achieved by the period 2008-12. The target of the protocol was to achieve a reduction of 5 per cent. However, the Kyoto Protocol was rejected by the US mainly for two reasons. *First,* it did not involve action on the part of major developing countries. *Second,* it was felt by the Bush administration that the Kyoto Protocol would be harmful to the US economy.

Bali Action Plan

The meeting which was held in December, 2008 in Bali, Indonesia adopted the 'Bali Action Plan'. The plan called upon the developed countries to draw up time bound GHG emission reduction targets and submit their achievements for monitoring, reporting and verification. The plan provides for financial and technical assistance by the developed countries to the developing countries.

Copenhagen Conference

In December, 2009, conference was held in Copenhagen in Denmark. A political agreement was reached between the US and the newly emerging major economies of Brazil, South Africa, India and China (BASIC). This agreement is known as the 'Copenhagen Accord' which recognises the sanctity of keeping global temperature rise to not more than 2 degrees Celsius. The accord was taken note of by other countries too and is expected to form the basis of further negotiations among nations this year.

The pledges were made to reduce and limit future emissions. The main one is bringing carbon neutrality by 2020. Which means reaching a point where the net emissions of GHGs are Zero. Developed countries insisted on developing countries to make absolute reductions of their emissions and monitor and verify the measures that the developing countries take to moderate their emissions. China and India resisted this. India made it clear that future negotiations should be based on equitable burden sharing as enshrined in the Kyoto Protocol and the Bali mandate.

The Indian environment minister Jairam Ramesh had some talks for the 20-25 per cent cut in carbon emission intensity by the year 2020 through a series of measures including mandatory fuel efficiency standards for vehicles, compulsory green building code and switching over to clean coal technologies, etc.

Suggestions to Overcome Climate Change

There are two approaches to reduce the impact of climate change. One is mitigation and the second is adaptation to climate change. Mitigation efforts attempt to prevent hazards from developing into disasters or reduce the effects of disasters when they occur. At present, two per cent of electricity is generated using fossil fuels and coal. Renewable energy sources such as solar energy, wind energy etc., can be used widely.

Migration of coastal population, increasing public transportation and forestry are the main adaptations that India can adopt. Today, only 12 per cent of the land is covered by the forests. Aforestation, Reforestation and protecting forests in the country would mitigate the climate change.

Usually people migrate from inland to coastal regions. With the rise in the sea level and coastal inundation, reverse migration may be suggested.

Emission can be controlled by regulations involving fixing limits and imposing penalties on infringements.

In order to control climate change, we need to reduce the use of fossil fuels like coal and oil and switch to green sources of energy like hydro power, nuclear energy, solar energy and wind energy. This would decrease the emission of GHGs substantially. Incentives may be given to promote to the use of clean fuel and technologies and penalise the use of carbon intensive fuels and technologies.

It is essential to create early warning systems and education for epidemic preparedness. Improved water and air pollution control would become essential for human health. Public awareness would be created for changes in personal behaviour. Training for researcher and health professionals can be given to stress the responsibility towards the expected outcome of Global Climate Change.

Conclusion

The urgent requirement is a holistic approach to mitigate climate change effects by all agencies and stakeholders through initiatives of awareness, training, capacity building and adopting more scientific approach towards development.

References

1. Velu Suresh Kumar (2010), "Climate Change: Its Impacts on India", *Southern Economist*, Vol. 49, No. 2, May 15, Bangalore.
2. Architesh Panda (2010), "Climate Refugees: Implications for India", *Economic and Political Weekly*, Vol. XLV, No. 20, May 5-21, Mumbai.
3. Madhu Verma and Munish Sikka, (2010), "Climate Change Mitigation through JFM in India", *Yojana*, Ministry of Information and Broadcasting, June, New Delhi.
4. Sungaraj A and Kumar D (2010), "Climate Change: Implications for Food Security in India", *Southern Economist*, Vol. 49, No. 6, July, 15, Bangalore.
5. Ravi Kumar K S., Priya Shyamsundar and Arivudai Nambi A (2010), "Economics of Climate Change Adaptation in India", *Economic and Political Weekly*, Vol. XLV, No. 18, May 1-7, Mumbai.
6. Krishnan N R, (2010), "Global Warming and Emission Control Role of Governments and Citizens", *Southern Economist*, Vol. 49, No. 4, June, 15, Bangalore.
7. Rajkumar Topandasani S (2010), "Global Warming and Sustainable Development", *Southern Economist*, Vol. 48, No. 24, June, 15, Bangalore.
8. Singh R. D., Manohar Arora and Rakesh Kumar, (2010), "Impact of Climate Change on Water Resources", *Yojana*, Ministry of Information and Broadcasting, July, New Delhi.
9. Gautam Dutt (2010), "Reaching A Climate Agreement: Beyond the Copenhagen Accord", *Economic and Political Weekly*, Vol. XLV, No. 17, April 24-30, Mumbai.
10. Dileep Kumar (2009), "Climate Change and Disaster Management", *Yojana*, Ministry of Information and Broadcasting, June, New Delhi.
11. Lakshmi R (2010), "Copenhagen Climate Conference", Kisan World, Vol. 37, No. 4, April, Chennai.
12. Anitha Selvaraj and Maheswari R (2008), "Impact of Global Warming on Global Economy", Kisan World, Vol. 35, No. 9, September, Chennai.
13. Neil Padukone (2010), "Climate Change in India: Forgotten Threats, Forgotten Opportunities", *Economic and Political Weekly*, Vol. XLV, No. 22, May 29-June4, Mumbai.

21

Climate Change and Food Security

Dr. K. Raja

Introduction

We are living at a moment in history that is unique with respect to the unprecedented progress in science, technology, and communication that has been achieved in the past three decades. Beginning with the Green Revolution of the 1970s, the information revolution of the 1980s, and the genetic revolution of the 1990s, the 20th century ended with the mapping of the human genome. The scientific and technological achievements are formidable accomplishments with significant potential for creating future sustainable and equitable well-being around the world. But today we live in a world of disparities, where a fifth of the global population lives in poverty and hunger.

Some 800 million people go hungry every day, and some 2 billion live on less than two dollars a day. Every minute of every day, 15 children and 15 adults die of hunger in the developing world. Without social, economic, and scientific progress, by the middle of the 21st century more than a third

Assistant Professor of Economics, Erode Arts College, Erode.

of the world's expected population of some 9 billion could be living in poverty. The poor are poor because they lack tangible assets, formal education, and technical skills, and have little access to health-care. Moreover, the poor are often discriminated against, both politically and socially.

Climate change is the most important global environmental challenge facing humanity with implications for food production, natural eco-systems, fresh water supply and health. The earth's climate system has demonstrably changed on both global and regional scales since the pre-industrial era. The unequivocal warming of the climate system is now evident from observations of increases in global average air and ocean temperatures, widespread melting of snow and ice, and rising global average sea level.

Global Environmental Change and Food Production

Food production systems interact with land resources, forest ecosystems, and bio-diversity. Maintaining the fertility and multi-functionality of soils, preserving genetic diversity, adopting effective water resources management and protection measures, and adapting to climate change are critical to enhancing agricultural production.

Climate change, air and water pollution, pests and diseases, economic and social turmoil, and even genetically modified crop contamination do not recognise or respect political and geographical boundaries. Without responsible decision-making, compromises, and even sacrifice, the children born in the wake of the 21st century may face a bleak future indeed. Global changes and challenges need to be considered because the actions taken-or not taken-today will affect the quality of life for generations to come. Two thirds of the world's population lives in areas that receive only one-quarter of the world's annual precipitation, while sparsely populated areas such as the Amazon Basin receive a disproportionately large share.

The growing water scarcity will pose a serious threat to food security, poverty reduction, human health, and protection of the environment. Thirty years ago, the world faced a global food shortage that some predicted would lead to catastrophic famines. The danger was averted because an international research effort enabled scientists to develop the farmers to adopt high-yielding varieties of major food crops. The lessons of that Green Revolution indicate that an integrated biological, environmentally sound, and socially viable strategy has to be at the core of the next precision green revolution.

Climate Change and Food Production

The Global Agro-ecological Assessment can provide a detailed understanding of the sensitivity of agricultural crops and regional land-use systems to climate change. The results of changes in cereal production in the 2080s based on three climate models-namely, the ECHAM 4 model of the Max-Planck Institute of Meteorology, the HADCM 2 model of the Hadley Centre for Climate Prediction and Research, and the CGCM 1 model of the Canadian Centre for Climate Modelling and Analysis-highlight that climate change will benefit the developed countries substantially more than the developing countries in terms of net gain in cereal production potential due to climate change.

Food Insecurity and Climate Change

Of the 117 developing countries in the world, some 94 countries account for 800 million undernourished people, as estimated by the FAO. Sixteen of these countries, each with a relatively high per capita gross domestic product of over US$ 3,000, are not considered. The total population of the remaining 78 countries, currently some 4.2 billion, is projected to increase to over 7 billion by 2050. In many of these countries more than two-thirds of the population derives their livelihoods from agriculture. Also, agriculture accounts for more than one-third of the total gross domestic product in these countries. The current food gap for the 780 million undernourished people in these countries is estimated to be in the order of 25 million tons, some 2.5 per cent of their total cereal production.

Many of these countries are poor, agriculture-based economies, often lacking the foreign exchange to finance food imports. Hence domestic production losses resulting from climate change will further worsen the prevalence and depth of hunger, and this burden will undoubtedly fall disproportionately on the poorest and the most vulnerable.

Issues

Global warming is likely to reduce agricultural production in the Tropics, where many developing countries are located. Policy options that could help farmers adapt to changing climates include encouraging agronomic research, providing irrigation or increasing its efficiency, maintaining or improving flood control, and facilitating human migration. Despite recent advances in analyzing the economic impacts of global warming, however, information about climatic threats to food security in developing countries is still extremely limited.

Over the past 250 years, deforestation, combustion of fossil fuels, and production of agricultural commodities such as rice and livestock have caused atmospheric concentrations of carbon dioxide (CO_2) and other greenhouse gases to rise significantly. 'Greenhouse' gases absorb energy radiated from Earth to space and warm the atmosphere. According to the Intergovernmental Panel on Climate Change (IPCC), increases in greenhouse gas emissions have been associated with an increase in the mean global temperature of 0.3°C-0.6°C since the late 19th century; by the end of the 21st century, according the IPCC, greenhouse gas emissions could cause the mean global temperature to rise by another 1.4°C-5.8°C. Increases in mean global temperature will have numerous effects on agricultural production, chief among them being changes in growing seasons-the length of time that soil temperature and soil moisture conditions are suitable for crop growth.

The U.S. Department of Agriculture's Economic Research Service (ERS) has developed a model that estimates the effects on world agriculture of climate-induced changes in growing seasons. The model links agricultural production to land classes defined by length of growing season. A geographical information system converts changes in temperature and precipitation generated by general circulation models of the atmosphere into changes in land classes.

Compared with 1990 economic conditions, the model shows that these land resource changes reduce agricultural output in equatorial regions where many developing countries are located.

Alternatives

Farmers and governments worldwide have several options to counter continued, long-run global warming. Farmer adaptations, such as switching crop varieties, introducing more suitable crops, or shifting from crops to grazing, can often be undertaken by individual farmers. Governments can provide reliable 6 to 8-month weather projections or information about suitable crop and livestock alternatives to help farmers increase production efficiency.

Climate Change and Food Security

Developed countries will largely benefit since cereal productivity is projected to rise in Canada, northern Europe and parts of Russia. In contrast, many of today's poorest developing countries are likely to be negatively affected in the next 50-100 years, with a reduction in the extent and potential productivity of cropland. Most severely affected will be sub-Saharan Africa due to its inability to adequately adapt through necessary resources or through greater food imports.

Problems facing farmers can be better understood if one considers the impact of climate change on weather or water precipitation, temperature and sunlight are the main factors behind agricultural production. Climate change can alter these factors causing essential threats to water availability, reduced agricultural productivity, spread of vector borne diseases to new areas, and increased flooding from sea level rise and even heavier rainfall. Climate variability is already the major cause of year-to-year fluctuations in production in both developed and developing countries.

Impact of Climate Change

Some of the impacts of climate change on food production include:

- Regional temperature rises at high northern latitudes and in the centre of some continents.

- Increased heat stress to crop and livestock; *e.g.*, higher night-time temperatures, which could adversely affect grain formation and other aspects of crop development.
- Possible decline in precipitation in some food-insecure areas such as southern Africa and the northern region of Latin America.
- Increased evapotranspiration rates caused by higher temperatures, and lower soil moisture levels.
- Concentration of rainfall into a smaller number of rainy events with increases in the number of days with heavy rain, increasing erosion and flood risks.
- Changes in seasonal distribution of rainfall, with less falling in the main crop growing season.
- Sea level rise, aggravated by subsidence in parts of some densely populated flood-prone countries, displacing millions.
- Food production and supply disruption through more frequent and severe extreme events.

Since food insecurity depends more on socio-economic conditions rather than on agroclimatic ones, the ways in which climate change can affect people's access to adequate food is rather complex. Future food security will mainly depend on the interrelationships between political and socio-economic stability, technological progress, agricultural policies and prices, growth of per' capita and national incomes, poverty reduction, women's education, trade and climate variability. Climate change, however, may affect the physical availability of food production by shifts in temperature and rainfall; people's access to food by lowering their incomes from coastal fishing because of rising sea levels; or lowering a country's foreign exchange earnings by the destruction of its export crops because of the rising frequency and intensity of tropical cyclones.

Some groups are particularly vulnerable to climate change: low-income groups in drought-prone areas with poor infrastructure and market distribution systems; low to medium-income groups in flood-prone areas who may loose stored food or assets; farmers who may have their land damaged or submerged by a rise in sea-level; and fishers who may loose their catch to shifted water currents or through flooded spawning areas. However, it is thought that by 2030 more countries will have improved their economies, infrastructure and institutions, and will be capable of compensating for the impact of climate change on domestic production through food imports.

Global Climate Change and Food Security in a Growing World

Global climate change is one of utmost international concerns. There is a perception among many that global climate change is simply global warming. In fact, global climate change is an integrated system of several atmospheric phenomena and their products.

Climate Change will Increase Hunger and Malnutrition

Climate change will worsen the living conditions of farmers, fishers and forest-dependent people who are already vulnerable and food insecure. Hunger and malnutrition will increase. Rural communities dependent on agriculture in a fragile environment will face an immediate risk of increased crop failure and loss of livestock. Mostly at risk are people living along coasts, in floodplains, mountains, drylands, and the arctic. In general, poor people will be at risk of food insecurity due to loss of assets and lack of adequate insurance coverage.

Climate Change will Particularly Affect Vulnerable People and Food Systems

More frequent and more intense, extreme weather will have adverse immediate impacts on food production, food distribution infrastructure, on livelihood assets and opportunities in both rural and urban areas. Changes in mean temperatures and rainfall, increasing weather variability and rising sea levels will affect the suitability of land for different types of crops and pasture, the health and productivity of forests, the incidence of pests and diseases, bio-diversity and eco-systems. Loss of arable land is likely due to increased aridity, groundwater depletion and the rise in sea level.

Fao's Role: Supporting those that are Least Likely to Adapt to Climate Change

Climate change adaptation requires the use of good agricultural, forestry and fisheries practices to meet changing and more difficult environmental conditions and the introduction of improved risk management measures. FAO's role is to promote the numerous adaptation options and assist rural communities in applying them. FAO provides a neutral forum for sharing information about best practices.

FAO works with governments, rural communities, research institutions and other bodies and provides global geo-spatial data, analytical tools and models, crop forecasting and impact monitoring and information' on risks related to climate variability and change. In Nigeria, at the request of the Ministry of Agriculture, FAO evaluated the impact of climate change on agriculture and food security. In Morocco, FAO contributed to a World Bank assessment study, covering climate change, agriculture and irrigation issues. In Bangladesh, F AO assists the Department of Agriculture and Extension in designing and implementing a project on how rural communities can adapt to climate change in drought prone areas.

Conclusion

Disruptions or declines in global and local food supplies due to climate change can be avoided through more efficient irrigation and watershed management, improved land cultivation and livestock management and the development of crop varieties and breeds that are adapted to changing climatic conditions. An effective use of climate data and forecasts, through early warning systems, can assist in analyzing the impacts of climate change on agricultural production and the entire food chain. For a country like India, sustainable agricultural development is essential not only to meet the food demands, but also for poverty reduction through economic growth by creating employment opportunities in non-agricultural rural sectors. There is a pressing need to strengthen the capacity of communities to cope effectively with both climatic variability and change.

Appropriate interventions are required to reduce the associated losses. For these, adequate measures will have to be strengthened both at the policy as well as the local level. In most cases these interventions would have to be very specific to the area at which it is being targeted depending on the nature of the problem being addressed.

22

Global Warming and Agricultural Sector

An Analytical Study on the Causes and Impact of Climate Change on Indian Agriculture

Dr. C. Rajendran

Climate change can manifest itself in gradual changes in temperature, precipitation and a rise in sea level, resulting in changes in frequency, intensity and duration of extreme events. Global warming means earth getting warmer and resulting in an ecological imbalance.

Climate change affects agriculture in different ways. Beyond a certain range of temperatures, warming tends to reduce yields. Evaporation from the soil leads to rising temperature and plants increase transpiration – that is, lose more moisture from their leaves. The combined effect is called 'evapotranspiration'. Seasonal changes in rainfall and temperature could impact agro-climatic conditions, planting and harvesting, water availability, etc. India, as a developing country has reasons to be concerned about the adverse impact of climate change on its economy. A large part of its population depends on climate sensitive sectors for livelihoods which makes it highly vulnerable to climate change. Climate change can have serious impact on its crops, forests, coastal regions

Assistant Professor, PG and Research Department of Economics, Government Arts College (Autonomous), Coimbatore - 641 018.

which can in turn affect the achievement of its important national development goals.

Causes of Global Warming

Global warming is increasing the earth's average temperature. The green house gases are the main culprits of the global warming. The green house gases like carbon dioxide, methane and nitrous oxide are playing hazards in the present time. These green house gases trap heat in the earth's atmosphere and thus result in increasing the temperature of the earth. The excessive emission of these gases is the major cause of global warming.

The major source of carbon dioxide is the power plants. These power plants emit large amounts of carbon dioxide produced from burning of fossil fuels for the purpose of electricity generations. Coal is the major fuel that is burnt in these power plants. Coal produces around 1.7 times as much carbon dioxide per unit of energy when flamed as does natural gas and 1.25 times as much as oil. Coal gives out 80 per cent more carbon per unit of energy it produces as compared to natural gas. Another major source of carbon dioxide in the atmosphere is the emission from the cars and other vehicles. About 20 per cent of carbon dioxide emitted in the atmosphere comes from burning of gasoline in the engines of the vehicles.

Buildings, both commercial and residential represent a large source of global warming pollution than cars and trucks. Building of these structures require a lot of fuel to be burnt which emits a large amount of carbon dioxide in the atmosphere. Cutting and burning of about 34 million acres of trees each year drastically increase warming. Trees collect CO_2 that we breathe out and they give back oxygen that we breathe in. Greater urbanisation, requirement of land for factories and buildings, requirement of timber are all reasons that are leading to deforestation which in turn lead to global warming.

Impact of Global Warming

Agriculture is the mainstay of Indian economy and provides food and livelihood security to a substantial section of the Indian population. The impact of climate change as witnessed in recent times has immense potential to adversely affect agriculture in this country. As a large part of the arable land in India is rain-fed, the productivity of agriculture depends on the rainfall and its pattern. Agriculture will be adversely affected not only by an increase or decrease in the overall amount of rainfall but also by shift in the timing of the rainfall. Any change in rainfall patterns poses a serious threat to agriculture, and therefore to the economy and food security.

The global warming increases the temperature and thus melting of the polar ice. There are frequent meltdown of glaciers that result in floods and other natural calamities. The melting of ice at the poles has led to increase in sea level which will engulf low lying countries. The effect of global warming is very evident on the animal kingdom. Some animals have become extinct due to loss of their natural habitat or their inability to evolve the rapid change in their life style because of the changes in the seasons. The migrating birds have changed their time to travel and also their place of migration.

The effects of global warming can be felt on the seasons too. There is shift in season cycle, as the summers are getting longer than the winters. This has affected the animals and made them to change their life style accordingly and those who failed to do so have perished or on the verge of extinction. Global warming is also responsible for the introduction of some new diseases. The bacteria are more effective and multiply much faster in warmer temperatures compared to cold temperatures. The increase in temperature has led to increase in the microbes that cause diseases.

Climate change is also affecting the crop production, as the crops are getting destroyed due to the sudden change in temperatures or sudden onset of rains. Also, the flash floods and other natural calamities affect the crop. It is a fact that because of global warming, the earth's atmosphere is getting more unpredictable with heavy rains in the areas which have scantly rainfall or drought in the areas which received good annual rainfall.

The impact of climate change on agriculture could result in water shortages and drought, new diseases, heat stress for animals. Scientists are studying very closely the effect of climate change in different fields including agriculture. Various studies have indicated that rise in temperature would affect the agricultural production. Indian agriculture, despite being a relatively minor contributor to greenhouse gas (GHG) emissions, will be a big loser if global temperatures rise.

The vulnerability of Indian agriculture to climate change is well acknowledged. But what is not fully appreciated is the impact, this will have on rain-fed (non-irrigated) agriculture, practiced mostly by small and marginal farmers who will suffer more. The crops that may be hit include pulses and oilseeds, among others. These are already in short supply and are consequently high priced. Nearly 80 million hectares, out of the country's net sown area of around 143 million hectares, lack irrigation facilities and hence, rely wholly on rain water for crop growth. Over 85 per cent of the pulses and cereals, more than 75 per cent of the oilseeds and nearly 65 per cent of cotton are produced from such lands. The crop yields are quiet low.

According to A. K. Singh, Deputy Director-General (Natural Resource Management) of the Indian Council of Agricultural Research (ICAR), medium-term climate change predictions have projected the likely reduction in crop yields due to climate change at between 4.5 per cent and 9 per cent by 2039.

The long-run predictions paint a scarier picture with the crop yields anticipated to fall by 25 per or more by 2099. This will have a detrimental effect on farmers' income and purchasing power, with obvious down-the-line repercussions. Though the rainfall records available with the Indian Meteorological Department (IMD) do not indicate any perceptible trend of change in overall annual monsoon rainfall in the country, noticeable changes have been observed within certain distinct regions.

At least three meteorological sub-divisions – *(i)* Jharkhand, *(ii)* Chhattisgarh and *(iii)* Kerala have shown significant decrease in seasonal rainfall though some others have recorded an uptrend in precipitation as well. Since, rain-fed crops like coarse grains, pulses and oilseeds are grown mostly during the kharif season, these are impacted by both low as well as excess rainfall. India is among countries most threatened by climate change with experts warning that rising temperatures will lead to more floods, heat waves, storms, rising sea levels and unpredictable farm yields. Here are the main potential effects of climate change on a country which is the world's seventh largest in area and is home to 1.1 billion people, a sixth of humanity.

The Food and Agricultural Organization (FAO) has warned that India could lose upto 125 million tonnes of cereals. The Intergovernmental Panel on Climate Change (IPCC) which was awarded Nobel Prize in the year 2008 has warned that due to global warming, the sea levels in Asia will rise by atleast 40cm by 2100 flooding vast areas on the coastline, including some of the most densely populated cities, whose population will be forced to migrate inland (The Hindu Business Line dated 03-11-2007). The first to be affected by the climate change will be those living in the fringe zones, working outdoors or whose livelihoods depend directly on the physical environment. Viewed from these perspectives, the main sectors facing risks from direct impact could be agriculture, water resources and health. If the present situation continues, in 2020 the food production will be reduced by 30 per cent and the heat will rise by 2.4 celcious degree (Dhinamalar, 2011).

The IPCC report indicates high probability of crop losses with increase in temperature in the tropical regions. Studies do confirm this trend. Among cereal crops important for food security, wheat is most sensitive to even small increase in temperature. Relatively, rice has greater tolerance to temperature increases. Increasing climate variability could result in considerable season/annual fluctuation in food production. All agricultural commodities are subject to such variability.

Solutions

The most important contributor to global warming is the increase in atmospheric CO_2 levels due to human activity. The following are the some of the suggestions to prevent global warming. CO_2 emission can be cut by reducing the use of fossil fuels by cutting back on car use, investing in energy efficiency, implementing energy conservation measures and utilising renewable resources such as wind, solar and hydropower. Reducing fossil fuel user will, coincidentally, also reduce emissions of methane, nitrous oxide and ozone.

Since CO_2 is consumed by plants and trees (known as carbon-sinks), reversing deforestation and implementing reforestation programmes may reduce levels in the atmosphere. The need to take such measures was first recognised at the RIO climate change convention in 1992, after which over 160 countries pledged to limit emissions of CO_2 and to protect and enhance natural 'sinks' of CO_2. Trees play a unique role in the global carbon cycle. They are the largest land-based mechanism for removing CO_2 from the air. Trees are able to store a large amount of CO_2 in their structure. An acre of forest will absorb about ten times the CO_2 amount absorbed by an acre of crop land. Planting more trees and reducing timber cut worldwide will help to restore the balance. Government should encourage the use of mass transit; provide tax rebates for people who buy low and no-pollution vehicles and subsidies to fossil fuel and the nuclear industries.

Green house gas emissions be managed using an incentive based policy, such as market based approach to capping and reducing such emissions. This type of strategy provides clear incentives for changes in business practices and the development of new technologies. It assures that economic forces are directed to keeping the cost of reducing emissions as low as they can be. Many industrial nations have now adopted policies intended to limit green house gases. Try to follow the environment-friendly policies like 'Reduce', 'Reuse' and 'Recycle'. Save containers, bags, everything that can be used in the future. Also we use cloth towels and napkins instead of paper ones and use rechargeable batteries instead of disposable ones. Try to minimize the usage of air conditioners, refrigerators and other electronic goods which cause hazardous effects to the mother earth and can maximize the usage of the solar energy and wind energy for the power generation.

Conclusion

Scientists are convinced that human actions are causing global warming. If this is so, it stands to reason that our own actions can also help to reduce this threat. Today global warming poses an extraordinary challenge. The world's leading atmospheric scientists tell us that a gradual warming of our climate is under way and will continue. This long-term warning trend poses even greater risks to many other nations, particularly poor countries that will be far less able to cope with a changing climate and low-lying countries where sea-level rise will cause significant damage.

Meeting the challenge of global warming will require sustained effort over decades on the part of Governments, who must establish the rules and modify them. Although much is being done to reduce the emission of green house gases, the efforts are still not enough. The Indian policy-makers must remember that climate change has a creeping effect on the economy and can further hurt the already fragile agricultural system.

References

1. International Panel on Climate Change (IPCC), *Fourth Assessment Report of the IPCC*, 2007 (http://www.ipcc.ch)
2. Christian Aid, 2007, *Human Tide: The Real Migration Crisis*, http://www.christianaid.org.uk
3. IPPC, 2007, *Climate Change 2007: Impacts, Adaptation and Vulnerability, Summary for Policy-makers* (http://www.ipcc.ch)
4. Stockholm Environment Institute, The World Conservation Union, the International Institute for Sustainable Development, World Watch Institute, 2007, *Adapting to Climate Change:*

Natural Resource Management and Vulnerability Reduction (http://www.wri.org)

5. United Nations Report 2007, *On Better Terms – A Glance at the Key Climate Change and Disaster Risk Reduction Concepts*, Consultation Version.
6. UNEP, 2007, *Adaptation to Climate Change Key Challenge for Artic People and Artic Economy*, Press Release April 2007 (http://www.unep.org)
7. UNEP, 2007, *Europe Set for Warmer Northern Winters, Hotter Southern Summers and Worsening Drought and Floods*, Press Release April 2007 (http://www.unep.org)
8. UNEP, 2006, *Deserts will Confront Growing Pressure in the Coming Decades*, – http://www.unep.org/geo/gdoutlook/007.asp
9. WWF, 2007, *Stormy Europe, the Power Sector and Extreme Weather*, http://www.wwf.org.uk
10. WWF, 2007, *Climate Change: Five Years Left to Change the World* (http://www.wwf.org.uk/news/n_0000003917.asp)
11. WWF, 2007, *Climate Change: Time to Prevent Biggest Disaster in History* (http://www.wwf.org.uk/news/n_0000003767.asp)
12. UNESCAP, 2000, *Climate Change and the Pacific Islands*, http://www.unescap.org/mced2000/pacific/background/climate.htm *Doc. 11476*
13. The Hindu Business Line, Daily Newspaper Dated 03-11-2007.
14. Dhinamalar, Daily Tamil Newspaper, Dated 03.02.2011, Covai Edition, p. 4.

Index

A

ADF, 140

ADT, 71

Agricultural challenges, 129-136

AIWC, 112

Amazon Basin, 169

Andhra Pradesh, 130, 132

Assam Branch Indian Tea Association, 133

Assam, 132

Atmosphere, 7, 88

Attenborough, David, 97

B

Bali Action Plan, 165

BASIC, 165

Bihar, 132

C

Carbon Disclosure Project, 156

Carbon emission, 137-145

Causes and effects of global warming, 32-39

- carbon content of fossil fuels, 35
- causes of global warming, 33
  - man-made causes, 34-35
  - natural causes, 33-34
- effects of global warming, 36-37
  - destruction of eco-systems, 36
  - disease, 36
  - storms and floods, 36-37
  - heat waves, 37
  - shrinking glaciers, 37
  - rising sea level, 37
- India initiatives, 37-38
- introduction, 32-33
- sources of anthropogenic methane emission, 35
- world CO_2, emission by source, 34

CFLs, 156

Chandrasekaran, S., 146

China, 7

Chloro Fluoro Carbons, 99, 152

Cholera, 99

Clean Air Act, 82

Clean Development Mechanism (CDM), 32

Climate change, 19, 63-76

Climate change and food security, 168-176

- alternatives, 172

climate change and food production, 170
climate change will
increase hunger and malnutrition, 174
particularly affect vulnerable people and food systems, 174-175
FAO role, 175
food insecurity and climate change, 170-171
global climate change and food security in a growing world, 174
global environmental change and food production, 169-170
impact of climate change, 172-174
introduction, 168-169
issues, 171-172
Copenhagen Summit, 135
Coral reefs, 134
Costa Rica, 78
Cyclones, 3

D

Deshpande, R S., 66
Devi, P. Ambiga, 152
Dhandapani, C., 157
Dhevarajan, PA., 77
Does carbon emission leads to economic growth rate in India, 137-145
Chakraborty, D., 138
co-integration rank test, 144
data and methodology, 139-144
Dinda, S., 138
review of the literature, 138-139
Domestic e-goods in global warming, 77-83
domestic e-goods, 81-82
duty of individual and government, 82
introduction, 77-78
marine degradation, 78-80
view of the skeptics, 82-83
Droughts, 3

E

Earth Summit, 3
ECM, 140
EKC, 137
Elango, D., 40
Empirical evidence of victimizing of India agricultural production by global warming, 40-46
climate change and agriculture, 41
global warming and India, 41-42
growth rate of output of various sub-sectors of agriculture in India, 45
India agricultural production, 44-46
introduction, 40-41
projected effects of global warming on India, 43-44
signs of global warming and climate change, 42-43
Environment friendly technologies to save climate, 47-53
carbon dioxide emissions, 52
carbon intensity, 50
sources of energy in India, 49

trends in fossil fuel use, 51
world energy supply, 2008, 28
Environmental awareness, 104-109
ERS, 171
European Union, 148

F

Famines, 78
FAO, 151, 175, 181
Floods, 3, 78
Food commodities, 65
Forests, 95
Fossil fuels, 127

G

Gandhimathi, S., 17
Gangotri glacier, 124
Gangotri glaciers, 8
GDP, 9, 13, 14, 63, 67, 98
Geetha, T.N., 110
Geethalakshmi, V., 67
GHG emission, 38, 98, 152
Global Climate Change, 165
Global efforts to control climate change, 157-167
causes for climate change, 159
emissions of GHG in India, 158
global efforts to control climate change, 164-165
green house effect, 158
impact of climate change, 159-164
introduction, 157-158
sources of green house gases, 158
suggestions to overcome climate change, 165-166
Global warming and agricultural challenges, 129-136
agricultural challenges, 131
climate change and agricultural sustainability, 133
false panacea, 135
India is unprepared, 134-134
introduction, 129-131
loss may amount to one third of total agri-production, 131-133
need of the hour, 135
rising sea levels due to global warming its impact on agriculture, 133-134
tea flavour fallout due to climate change, 133
Global warming and agricultural sector, 177-184
causes of global warming, 178
impact of global warming, 178-181
solutions, 182-183
Global warming and its effects on human health, 97-103
effect of
disasters, 100-102
floods, 100
hot climate, 99-100
increasing air pollution, 100
global warming on human health, 98-99
global warming in India, 98
Global warming and the initiatives of environmental awareness, 104-109
acid rain, 106

climate change, 105
loss of tropical forests, 106
objectives, 107-108
attitude, 107
awareness, 107
evaluation ability, 107
knowledge, 107
participation, 107
skill, 107-108
ozone layer, 105
public awareness, 107

Global Warming, 26, 32-39, 40-46, 77-83, 88, 130, 152-156
earth water resources, 5-9
green house effect, 3-4
hydrological cycle, 4
impacts of global warming, 153-155
introduction, 1-3
social and economic effect, 9

GNP, 21, 138
Gobi, S., 84
Gomathi, K.R., 152
Government of India, 139
Gramin Shakti, 112
Green House Gases (GHGs) , 33, 48
Green India, 38
Green Revolution, 168
technologies, 73
GSDP, 68
GSP, 138

H

Health and environment problems, 59
Hindus, 43
Human Development Report, 118
Human health, 97-103

I

IARI, 21, 42
ICAR, 84
IIT, 67
Impact of climate change on agricultural production at global level and in India, 17-25
case study on the effect of climate change on agricultural production in India, 23-25
climate change and agricultural production at global level, 19-21
climate change and agricultural production in India, 21
models used to predict climate change by the Indian agricultural research institute, 21-22
predicted climate change effects on agriculture, 22
rice production, 22-23
what are the policy implications of these predictions, 23
wheat production, 22

Impact of climate change on paddy production, 63-76
application of inputs in paddy cultivation, 72-74
discussion and interpretation of regression results, 74-75
introduction, 63-64
policy implications for decision-makers, 75-76
review of related literature, 64-68

scenario of paddy production in Tamil Nadu, 70-72
state of Tamil Nadu, 68-70
Impact of global warming and economic development, 11-16
forecasting emissions growth and its impact, 13-15
global warming, 13
introduction, 11-12
policy instruments for global warming, 12-13
Impact of global warming in economic development, 122-128
global warming and
agriculture, 126
economic growth, 127
economic inequality, 127-128
health, 128
marine production, 127
natural calamities, 126-127
problems of global warming, 124-125
types of environmental damages, 125-126
air pollution, 125
noise pollution, 125-126
soil pollution, 126
water pollution, 125
what is global warming, 123
Impact of global warming on agricultural production, 146-151
how climate affects agriculture, 147
impact of climate change in agriculture, 150-151
impact on
agriculture, 148-149
crop yields, 147-148
measures undertaken to mitigate global warming, 155
suggestions, 155-156
Impacts of global warming, 26-31
dangerous weather patterns, 29
destroying earth, 29
economic consequences, 28-29
effects on animals, 30
full effects on humans, 30-31
hostile planet for our children, 30
impact on agriculture, 27
impact on food security, 29-30
impact on health, 27
melting glaciers, 28
ocean acidification, 28
polar melting, 27-28
sea level rise, 28
Indian Agriculture Research Institute, 161
Indian Economic Survey, 139
Indian Economy, 67
Indian Express, 89
Indian global warming and climate change in agricultural production, 84-96
agriculture, 89-95
global warming
and climate change, 86-87
India, 85-86
introduction, 84-85
social effects of climate change in India, 87-88

sustainable development, 88-89
Indian Meterological Department, 180
Indian ocean, 38
Industrial Revolution 47, 129
INFOCANE, 21
INFOCROP, 21
INFORSE, 112
INSEDA, 112
Integrated Cereals Development Programme in Wheat, 85
International Emission Trading (IET), 32
IPCC, 2, 64, 151, 181
IPCC Third Assessment Report, 19
Irrigation, 42

J

Jayalakshmi, V.P., 47
Joint Implementation, 32
Jowar crop, 25

K

Kubendran, A., 11
Kumar, A. Senthil, 122
Kyoto Protocol, 3, 118

L

Lavanya, V.L., 97
LFG, 57

M

Malaria, 42
Malarvizhi, V., 32
Manonmani, M., 26
Mars, 1
Meera, N., 54
Millennium Development Goals, 117
Montana Glacier National Park, 37
Municipal Solid Waste, 60
Muniyandi, B., 84
Muthukumar, P., 104

N

National Action Plan on Climate Change, 37
National Agricultural Insurance Scheme, 76
National Food Security Mission, 85
National Oceanic and Atmospheric Administration, 153
National Rural Employment Guarantee Scheme (NREGS), 75
National Solar Mission, 38
National Water Mission, 38
NGOs, 119

O

OECD, 138
OECD countries, 50

P

Palanisami, A., 63
Plight of Indian farmers, 134
Poverty, 47, 128

R

Rain, 7
Raja, K., 168
Rajam, V., 32
Rajendran, C., 177
Renukanthan, V.S., 137
Rice production, 66
River Cauvery, 64
River Colorado, 37
River Ganga, 8, 37

Runn of Kutch, 43

Russian Federation, 51

S

Sarathy, T., 129

Saravanadevi, N., 129

Science express, 65

SELCO, 112

SEWA, 112

Shobha, K, 152

Solar Electric Light Fund (SELF), 111

Solid waste and climate change in India, 54-62

climate change and solid waste, 59-61

methods of solid waste management in some major cities in India, 55-59

solid waste generation, 54-55

SRI, 71

Sun, 1

T

Thirukkural, 132, 135

TIDE, 112

Tornados, 78

U

UKMO, 20

UN Framework Convention on Climate Change, 52

UN Human Rights Council, 121

UN World Resource Index, 124

UN WRI, 127

UNESCO, 107

UNFCC, 37

United Nations Climate Change Conference, 119-120, 135

United Nations Environment Programme, 33

United Nations Framework Convention on Climate Change, 3

Universe, 77

Urban planning, 103

Uttarakhand, 42

V

VECM, 140

Vijayakumar, K.S., 1

VOCs, 80

W

Waste prevention and recycling, 61

WEDO, 116, 118, 119

WHO, 99, 114, 163

Women role in a warming world, 110-121

absence of women in global environment policy, 117

climate change is not gender neutral, 115-116

current status in the field of renewable energy in India, 113-114

energy is a human right, 111-112

engaging women on adaptation strategies, 116-117

fighting climate change and involving women, 118

going forward, 120

how and why renewable energy is important for women, 112-113

introduction, 110-111

other green power alternatives, 118-119

progress in the UNFCCC, 119-120

solar energy does actually prevent global warming, 114

women role in the clean energy economy, 114-115

World Bank, 155

World Health Organization (WHO), 36

WTO, 114